ADVANCED RACE WALKING

ADVANCED RACE WALKING

The Serious Race Walker's Guide to Competitive Success

Martin Rudow

Head Coach, U.S. National Men's Race Walking Team

**Funding by The Athletics Congress
and John MacLachlan**

Technique Publications
Seattle, Washington

Library of Congress cataloging in publication data available.
First printing 1987 10 9 8 7 6 5 4 3 2 1

Design and Production by Laing Communications Inc., Bellevue, Washington

Editorial Coordination— Delia Howard
Design and Layout— Sandra J. Harner
Production Coordination— Bonnie F. Ricciardelli
Cover Illustration— Chuck Solway
Interior Illustrations— Dale Davis
Photography— Wayne Glusker, Tom Carroll, Martin Archambault, Judy Rudow

Technique Publications
4831 NE 44th
Seattle, Washington 98105

Printed in the U.S.A.

Contents

Foreword

Advanced Race Walking is written for a select audience— competitive race walkers. There are only a few thousand people around the world who race walk in competition, as compared to the estimated 20,000,000 who walk regularly for fitness.

Why, then, have I spent months of my life researching and writing a book which inevitably will reach a very small audience? The reason is simple: I love the sport of race walking. During the 2½ decades I've been involved with the sport as a competitor, judge and coach, I have enjoyed a rare camaraderie with some of the finest people I could ever hope to know.

My close involvement with the U.S. Race Walking Team in the past few years has made it even more apparent how much a book which deals exclusively with the competitive aspects of the sport is needed. *Advanced Race Walking* is written in response to this need, with the aim of providing race walkers with vital information and inspiration to help them reach their goals.

Hopefully, *Advanced Race Walking* will also clear away several misconceptions about race walking, and help to earn its athletes the respect that they deserve. Race walking is a demanding and difficult event. Competitive race walkers train as hard as any serious athlete, and are equally as dedicated. The sport is not an esoteric pursuit followed only by an eccentric few; rather, race walking belongs in the mainstream of track and field athletics.

With the increasing worldwide participation in competition and exposure as a worthwhile fitness activity, the interest in race walking is growing constantly. I trust that *Advanced Race Walking* will only help move this welcome process forward.

Martin Rudow

Acknowledgements

I have been involved in the sport of race walking for more than 25 years. Throughout this time, several people have been especially helpful in developing my ideas on training and technique. Although some of their methods are now outdated, this book would have been impossible to write without their inspiration and suggestions over the years. Don Jacobs, Bob Hendrickson, Ron Laird, Bob Bowman, Jerzy Hausleber, Bruce McDonald, Larry Young and Frank Alongi deserve my recognition and the thanks of everyone who benefits from this book.

Special thanks should also be extended to a few key people whose last-minute contributions add a great deal to the quality of the finished product. They include Karen Clippinger-Robertson, Dr. John Robertson, and Gary Westerfield. I also wish to thank John MacLachlan, who provided the initial support for this book and whose patience, I hope, has been rewarded.

Advanced Race Walking could not have been written without the patience of my family. To them—Judy, Kurt and Matt—this book is dedicated.

Chapter I

How to Use this Book

Do not skip this page! If you have read even this far, you are obviously seriously interested in pursuing success in competitive race walking. So, do not jump right to the training sections ... it is essential that you read *every* section consecutively in order to learn the reasons behind the training schedules and technique pointers described in this book. If you must skip to the training tables, be sure to read over the chapters preceding them as soon as possible.

Success in race walking depends on the development of five areas. Each training session outlined in this book is geared to improving one or more of these capabilities. These five areas for improvement are:

1. Technique
2. Endurance
3. Speed
4. Flexibility
5. Strength

Assuming that general health is good, a walker should prioritize specialized training in roughly this order—that is, placing primary importance on technique and the least emphasis on strength. Following a brief definition of race walking rules and competitive opportunities, *Advanced Race Walking* devotes one chapter to each of these five capabilities, explaining the rationale for the training methods which are recommended. Summaries are provided where necessary to highlight the most important advice in each chapter.

Advanced Race Walking is written mainly for the self-coached athlete, or those who are trained by inexperienced coaches ... in other words, for the majority of English-speaking race walkers. Non-technical language is used to provide a clear understanding of the principles of training, and how to apply these principles in training and racing. Words that are perhaps unfamiliar to some have been italicized, referring the reader to the glossary which has been included to define the occasional technical terms.

The training tables themselves will guide the walker in preparing a goal-oriented, progressive training program. The schedule is based on ideal conditions and naturally will prove difficult to follow exactly, due to the likelihood of some interruptions such as injuries and inclement weather. By paying close attention to the basic principles of training, however, you can easily adapt these training tables to your own situation.

Race walking is a sport that is constantly in transition. Rule changes may occur that will render parts of the material in this book outdated. But for now, *Advanced Race Walking* represents the most up-to-date information available for success in our sport. Please use this book as it was intended and ensure the maximum reward for your efforts. Good Luck!

Chapter II

Race Walking by Definition

Race walking has been a part of the international track and field calendar since the 1906 Olympic games. The sport has experienced swings in popularity and participation during its history, but recently has seen more international participation than ever before— perhaps fueled by the increasing interest in fitness around the world. Many nations, including emerging track and field powers such as China and several third world countries (notably Mexico and Columbia), are fielding strong teams which compete seriously with traditional walking powers, such as the U.S.S.R. and Italy.

Race walking competition, like other track and field events, is governed by the International Amateur Athletic Federation (I.A.A.F.), which dictates the rules of legal race walking. These rules have changed somewhat over the years, and more changes in the future are possible. As of 1987 the I.A.A.F. defines race walking as:

" ... progression by steps so taken that unbroken contact with the ground is maintained. At each step, the advancing foot of the walker must make contact with the ground before the rear foot leaves the ground. During the period of each step when a foot is on the ground, the leg must be straightened (i.e., not bent at the knee) at least for one moment, and in particular, the supporting leg must be straight in the vertical upright position."

Failure to walk with at least one foot on the ground at all times is known as *lifting.* This violation occurs when the toe of the supporting foot leaves the ground before the heel of the advancing foot makes contact, resulting in a loss of the *double contact* or *double support phase.* Failure to straighten the knee as it passes under the body's center is known as *creeping.*

The I.A.A.F. also rules how walking races shall be conducted, including the action of the judges. Judging is an important part of competitive race walking, since an athlete may be completely disqualified from a competition for failing to walk as defined by the I.A.A.F. rules stated above.

No matter how strong a walker is, regardless of rigorous training programs and support from countrymen, if a competitor cannot walk legally, he or she cannot win a race walking event. One of the main purposes of this book is to help walkers master this art.

Chapter III

Competitive Opportunities

Race walking offers male athletes a chance to compete for the greatest prize of all—an Olympic gold medal. Competitions in the Olympic games are held at both 20 kilometers (12.4 miles) and 50 kilometers (31 miles). Race walking for women seems certain to be added to the Olympic calendar as early as 1992, probably at a distance of 10,000 meters (6.2 miles).

Both men and women compete in the world's next largest and well-publicized track and field event, the World Track and Field Championships. Like the Olympic games, these championships are held every four years. Men again compete in the 20 and 50 kilometer events, while women race the 10,000 meter distance.

A World Indoor Track and Field Championship meet has recently been added to the athletic calendar, featuring a 3,000 meter event for women and a 5,000 meter event for men. This competition will be held regularly, but is still in the formative stages and the exact dates of future meets is unclear.

For race walking purists, perhaps nothing equals the excitement of race walking's own World Cup—a weekend event held every two years in which men compete for the Lugano Trophy and women for the Eschborn Cup. The Lugano Cup is contested at two distances—20 and 50 kilometers–while women race in the 10,000 meter event. The emphasis of this weekend is on team competition, with five athletes representing each country. The Lugano and Eschborn races offer rising athletes their best chance at an international berth.

The World Junior Track and Field Championship was inaugurated in 1986 and is also held every two years. This competition includes a 10,000 meter walk for junior men and junior women. Intercollegiate competition is limited to the National Association of Intercollegiate Athletics

(N.A.I.A.) track and field program at the 10,000 meter distance.

Every country that maintains an established walking program holds youth walks for defined age groups as part of their developmental program. In the United States walkers as young as nine years of age can compete in short track walks locally, and older junior walkers can qualify for national competitions for their age groups and for Junior Olympic walks. Masters also compete in their own class of events, including walks in the Senior Olympics, a major event for the over-40 set.

In short, race walking offers an enormous amount of opportunity for those seriously attempting a career in athletics. Whether an athlete is interested in international track and field championships or local age-group and all-comers meets, race walking provides excellent opportunities for each scope of competition.

Chapter IV

Training for Technique

Although a competitive race walker may actually spend more *time* training for endurance, strength and speed, "good technique" must be the primary goal of a race walking training program, and all else must be secondary to that goal. In modern race walking competition, this does not necessarily mean achieving impeccably legal and classic style. Rather, good technique means the style which results in a fast time without disqualification and allows a walker to train and race without injury.

Besides the most obvious reason for good technique— to avoid outright disqualification— there are other equally good reasons for walkers to place technique training at the top of their priority list:

- Good technique is energy-efficient, less tiring and less stressful on the body than poor technique.
- Good technique allows walkers to use all of their speed and strength in a race rather than hold back for fear of disqualification. If proper technique is maintained, walkers can use every bit of power they possess— as opposed to those competitors who complain after a race that they "could have gone faster, but were afraid of the judging."

Good technique must be developed even at the temporary expense of other training. To illustrate this point, consider a world-class 10,000 meter runner who is making a mid-career change to race walking. His nervous and muscular/skeletal systems are developed for running. If we could chart this athlete's present level of conditioning and technique, the graph (A) would appear as shown on the following page.

Because the athlete's poor technique puts him in constant danger of disqualification, he must concentrate on race walking technique training at the expense of further conditioning routines. The graph now begins to change (B):

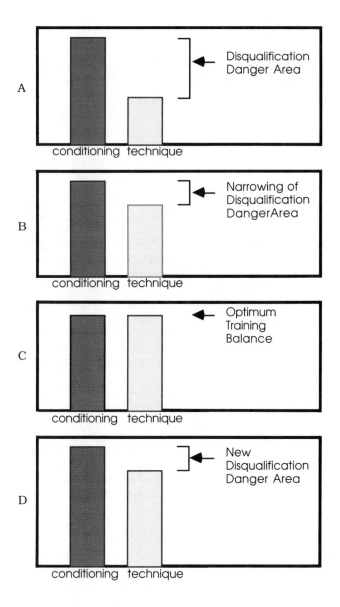

Finally, after continued technique training, significant progress can begin (C). The ex-runner's technique has now improved to the point where further technique training is needed only to maintain the good habits that he has developed. Future training can be as hard as it was during the athlete's running career, or even harder, but additional work now reinforces good technique while improving strength and speed.

Needless to say, few walkers start out as world class 10,000 meter runners. But *all* walkers must continually upgrade their technique as their conditioning improves or they increasingly risk disqualification (D).

Progressive Stress Adaptation

Throughout the book, we will continually refer to the process of *progressive stress adaptation* as the basis for improvement in technique, as well as improvement in endurance, speed, strength and flexibility. This process was first described by Dr. Hans Selye in his classic book, *The Stress of Life.* To summarize progressive stress adaptation in simple terms, an athlete stresses his or her body during training, and through these workouts gradually forces the body to adapt to this stress. The adaptation allows the athlete to gain strength and flexibility, and increase endurance to handle greater workloads of a similar type.

When joints, muscles and connective tissue are stressed during technique training, the body reacts by building new capillary networks around these stressed areas. The new capillary networks supply more blood and can carry off more wastes, allowing the joints and muscles to work efficiently for a longer period of time and over a wider range of motion than before.

This adaptation through capillary build-up is one of the best reasons to follow activity-specific training programs. Because athletes involved in other sports have not concentrated on developing the muscular strength and endurance in the areas essential to race walking, they usually cannot race walk with a legal style. For the same reason, race walking technique cannot be improved with a training program that largely recommends running, for example. The goal of progressive stress adaptation in improving technique is to build strength, endurance and flexibility in the areas of the body that are most stressed by correct technique.

The Basics of Race Walking Movement

Before concentrating on the individual elements of proper technique and how these components work together, it is important to understand and visualize the

basic movements of the body during race walking.
Everyone's hips, for instance, rotate as they walk. To
illustrate this point, try this simple test: Stand up and
place your finger tips on the ball-and-socket joint of each
hip. As you walk forward, you will notice that your fingers
rotate forward and slightly downward with the hip joints.
In race walking, this forward rotation becomes faster as
stride length and the range of motion increase. As with
most elements of race walking style, you simply are
accelerating a natural movement of the body and covering
a wider range of motion with this movement.

Arm action can be similarly demonstrated. The rapid
arm swing, so familiar in race walking, is a completely
natural motion. Pay close attention to the arm swing that
you use when walking normally. As the right arm swings
forward, the left leg comes forward. Your lead foot strikes
the ground just as your lead hand stops swinging forward.
In race walking, however, the arms are bent at a 90° or
sharper angle and the range of arm motion is increased.

Keep these basic principles in mind as we detail the
individual elements of correct race walking style.
Remember that when put into practice, these elements
must work together. It is difficult to walk with truly
good technique as long as any of these areas need
improvement.

The Elements of Race Walking Technique
Posture

The torso should remain in an upright position at all
times during the stride, leaning forward up to 5° during the
propulsive stage. This lean must come from the heels—
never as a result of bending forward at the waist. This
correct forward lean will help the body derive maximum
forward pushing thrust from the rear foot.

Developing and then holding this proper lean will help
keep the body in correct alignment, with the hips, waist,
and rib cage forming a straight line, even when bending
forward. Avoid letting the hips or rib cage fall behind the
waist since this will interfere with "connectiveness" of the
torso and hips with resulting loss of power.

Leaning *too* far forward (more than 5°) is also a
problem, even if this lean develops from the heel. An
extreme forward lean causes a walker to land flat-footed
and pull the rear foot off the ground before it rolls up on the

toes. A high risk of disqualification exists when a walker leans too far forward at high speed.

Head Carriage

Because the head accounts for as much as 10 percent of the body's mass, it can have a major effect on technique. Ideally, a walker should carry the head at a natural level, neither dropping it too far forward or holding it too far back. The eyes should focus on a spot at least four meters (12 feet) in front of the body.

Dropping the head forward causes upper body tension and rolls the shoulders high and forward. These factors can bring the hips through too high, and cause the walker's lead foot to flatten prematurely as it makes contact with the ground. A premature snatching away of the rear foot may also occur, creating a complete loss of the double contact phase. Holding the head too far back also creates upper body tension, but is not as likely to cause a disqualification problem.

Shoulder and Upper Torso Action

In all athletic events, a relaxed upper body is the key to powerful, coordinated body movements. This fact can be observed in any form of sporting competition; the best shooters in basketball, the most successful receivers in football, the outstanding hitters in baseball, are always the athletes who seem the most relaxed and make their sport look effortless. This relaxation begins with the upper body.

In race walking, a rigid upper body limits arm motion and tends to restrict hip motion. A short and

Contrast the way these two walkers are using their upper bodies. The walker on the right is showing excessive lateral arm motion, a high hip carriage and tight, rigid shoulders. The walker on the left is driving the arms low along the waistband and demonstrating greater overall coordination with his hips and shoulders.
(Photo by Wayne Glusker.)

inefficient stride, upper body fatigue and an increased danger of lifting result. Tension, whether from competition or outside stress, is often a major cause of rigid upper body action. Simply relieving stress in everyday life and consciously relaxing the shoulders and neck when they feel "tight" are basic and important ways to achieve relaxed, fluid upper body movements.

As the arms are swung forward and backward, low over the waistband, the shoulder and upper torso must turn with them. Although this movement is subtle, developing such coordination is important since the muscles of the upper torso— the serratus, the latissmus dorsi and the lower trapezius— are critical in arm extension and retraction. Walkers who turn only the tops of their shoulders, or whose shoulders remain completely rigid, are not using these muscles and rob themselves of extension and power. To achieve the proper torso and shoulder coordination, walkers should work to achieve a sensation of using the muscles under the armpit and concentrate on the upper body flexibility exercises in chapter 6, "Training for Flexibility".

Arm Action

In order to achieve correct arm action, the arms must work with the shoulders and upper torso, and these parts should be thought of as one unit. Working the arms through the correct range of motion and driving them low over the waistband both contribute to powerful walking.

The ideal range of arm motion is the same for all race walkers and can be described exactly. Walkers must discipline themselves to walk within this range of motion during all training and racing, while developing as much power and speed as possible. The ability to keep arm and shoulder action under control, despite high speed and fatigue, is the secret to walking fast, legal times.

Here is a method to find your own correct range of arm motion: First, put on an old white t-shirt. Using a large felt-tipped marker, draw one line right down your sternum and another one across the nipple line. These lines cross to form a "t" at the level where your hands should reach when swinging forward. The hands should never swing above the horizontal line of the "t", but swing to a point about six inches directly in front of your chest at the crossing of the "t." The right hand should never cross over to the left side of the vertical "t" line, and vice versa.

There is a direct relationship between range and angle of arm swing and stride length. As we discussed in the

This walker is not deriving any power from his arm action. The elbow should remain at waistband level, with the elbow and forearm at a 90° angle.
(Photo by Tom Carroll.)

basics of race walking movement, as long as the leading arm is being driven forward, the opposite leading leg will be driving forward. Unless it is done intentionally, the leading heel will not make contact with the ground until the leading arm stops its forward swing. And, as long as the rear arm is being driven backward, the rear or trailing leg will remain on the ground.

A powerful low and controlled arm swing will produce the exact same characteristics in the stride. Short, choppy arm swings, resulting in rigid shoulder and hip movements, produce a short stride. Long, slow arm swings result in "slow feet," overstriding and poor knee straightening action. Excessive side-to-side arm swings result in excessive side-to-side hip swings and a shortening of the stride. Understanding this arm-leg relationship is critical to understanding the importance of the proper range of arm motion.

Many people believe, incorrectly, that the key to fast race walking lies in increasing stride length or being born with long legs. How many times have we heard, "So-and-so must be a good race walker since he's got such long legs."? However, the key to gaining leg speed is using the proper stride length for your own body and increasing the number of strides per minute. And the *best* way to find this proper stride length is to control arm action and work arm swing within its ideal range of motion.

Carrying the hands in the most effective position is also an important part of correct arm action. As those

During the 1985 Lugano Cup, a group of the world's top 20 kilometer walkers generally exhibit relaxed upper bodies and low, powerful arm carriage. (Photo by Martin Archambault.)

involved in the martial arts know, a loosely clenched fist, with the thumb on top, is most effective in generating power as the driving arm passes along the waistband. Avoid walking with the palms facing up or allowing the hands to flap. Sloppy hand action, which angles the force away from the body and lengthens the arm, results in a loss of power in the arm drive.

It is critically important to keep the arms low as they are driven back-and-forth at the hips. As the arms swing through, the hands, forearms and elbows should continually pass the body at the waistband—neither above nor below it. The hands should reach no further than the back of the buttocks on the arms' back-swing. You can monitor this action by having someone watch your hands as you race walk past them. This person should not be able to see the hand of your far arm swing behind your buttocks as that arm swings backward.

During the arm swing, the elbows should remain bent at an angle of 90° or sharper. The elbows must swing through low at the waistband level, reaching this level as a result of relaxed shoulder and upper torso action— *not* by swaying the trunk from side-to-side. Drive the elbow straight back and avoid "chicken winging" or letting the rear elbow angle out to the side.

Even sloppy and basically incorrect arm action often can be tolerated if the elbows swing through low, the shoulders remain relaxed and the actions of each arm are identical. In short, be consistent and strive for balanced motion. The right elbow should swing through at the same level as the left, the left hand should reach the same point in front of your body as the right and so on.

Hip Action

As discussed earlier, even untrained walkers will increase the rotation of their hips if they try to walk faster. The hip rotation consists of two simultaneous actions— one that is vertical and the other horizontal.

The horizontal action is the most obvious. The leg and hip should move forward and backward horizontally, with a minimum of side-to-side movement. The hip also should move vertically, dropping as the leg swings forward, reaching its lowest point when the driving foot is directly under the hip, or when the advancing foot passes next to the supporting leg. Although the hip can be driven through horizontally without vertical movement, this action is less efficient and the resulting high hip carriage causes the driving foot to swing through too high from the ground. These actions often lead to lifting and a percussive impact as the driving foot strikes the ground.

Contrast the techniques of the walkers shown here. On the right, Josef Pribilnec's superior forward lean and hip drop offer greater extension and legality than the technique of the walker on the left. This walker's rigid body carriage and high hip drive severely limit legal stride length.
(Photo by Martin Archambault.)

Proper horizontal and vertical hip motion can add as much as 20 centimeters to each stride. Such an increase in stride length cannot be achieved through any other technique adjustment without running a high risk of disqualification. This hip motion is the single most important element of technique that separates race walking from regular walking.

Long-time runners who attempt race walking very often display little horizontal or vertical hip movement, but are able to walk at a fast tempo by relying on leg strength and cardiovascular conditioning. However, they simply cannot walk beyond a certain pace legally until they master this very important element of race walking technique.

Leg Action

A walker's speed depends upon the length of stride and the *strike rate*, or frequency with which the feet hit the ground. As explained earlier, it is a common misconception that long legs or a long stride are prerequisites for superior race walking speed. A high strike rate is the real key to attaining this speed. The walker who is able to maintain a very high strike rate, while observing the rules of correct technique, will consistently reach outstanding speeds with acceptable legality. The great Mexican walker, Daniel Bautista, may have been the fastest walker of all time although he stood only 5'5".

The important principles of leg action in race walking are:

1. One leg (the supporting leg) remains on the ground while the other leg (the swinging or driving leg) swings forward.
2. The supporting leg also becomes the pushing leg as the center of gravity passes over it and the walker applies the all-important forward push as soon as the foot of the supporting leg is flattened.
3. The double contact phase occurs during the brief instant when both feet are on the ground. This phase keeps the walker's body level. A bobbing of the walker's head is the most obvious sign that contact is not being maintained.

Remember that mastering correct arm action is critical to attaining correct stride length, because the two elements are directly related. Avoid reaching out with the lead foot to increase stride length; the area in front of the body is basically "dead space" since the walker is unable to push from this region.

Rudy Haluza, one of the United States' all-time greatest walkers, demonstrates powerful, high-speed, leg action during the 1968 Olympic games. Note that both knees are bent—one propelling, the other driving and the ankle of the pushing leg is flexing to provide maximum forward thrust. (Photo by Tom Carroll.)

Knee Action

According to the rules of race walking, the supporting knee must be straightened as it passes under the body's center. In years past this rule was often taken to mean that the supporting leg should be straightened as soon as the leading foot made contact with the ground. The term, "locked knee," was used to describe the desired knee straightening.

Modern technique, however, allows a much more flexible approach to knee straightening. Upon impact, the supporting knee should be relaxed instead of locked, and may even be noticeably bent. In either case, the knee definitely must be straightened as it passes under the body's center, but the joint should still be relaxed—again, not "locked." Slightly tensing the quadraceps will help prevent knee joint fatigue and lessen the chances of injury, while still allowing the walker to comply with the straightening rules.

This modern or soft-knee technique may cause problems if the judging is overly strict. A walker attempting to master the soft-knee technique should work with an experienced judge as much as possible to assure that he or she is still satisfying the straightening rules.

The length of time that a walker should hold the knee straightened is a matter of some debate. Traditionally, walkers have kept the knee of the supporting leg straight as long as possible, driving back through the knee and calf to exert forward propulsive force. Bending the knee sooner is also an acceptable technique and may reduce the strain on the joint. Walkers with a history of knee trouble would be well-advised to try this approach.

Carl Schueler's relaxed distance technique brought him to a sixth place finish in the 50 kilometer race of the 1984 Olympic games. Note the relaxed upper body, and proper forward lean and knee straightening technique. (Photos by Tom Carroll.)

In addition to straightening, correct knee action also requires a low, driving hip movement. If the hip is rotating properly in the vertical and horizontal planes, the low, forward driving action of the knee will come naturally. High hip carriage will result in a high knee drive (and in turn results in a high foot drive). These movements give the walker's style a "joggy" look, attracting unwelcome attention from the judges and serving as an indicator of potentially injurious style problems elsewhere.

Foot Action

As defined by the rules of legal race walking, the toe of the rear foot must not leave the ground until the heel of the advancing foot has made contact with the ground. This period, the double contact phase, may last for only a fraction of a second in high-speed walking.

If the shoulders and hips are being utilized properly, moving vertically as well as horizontally, the lead foot should skim the ground as it passes by the supporting leg. As the heel of this foot touches the ground in front of the body, the forefoot should form a 90° angle with the tibia (front shinbone). This 90° angle allows the walker to add a few centimeters to each step without overstriding, proving to be the most efficient technique. (Walkers with chronic shin problems may need to adopt a more flat-footed approach to relieve strain on the tibia.) If the foot is being driven through low as a result of low knee drive and proper vertical hip rotation, there will be minimal percussive force and braking action as the foot makes contact with the ground.

Upon the lead foot's landing, the *single contact phase* begins. The foot rolls down smoothly, kept from flopping using ankle strength. The foot should flatten completely only as it passes under the body's center of gravity. If a walker's foot flattens before passing this point, no pushing power can be applied and forward propulsion is temporarily halted.

As soon as the foot is flattened, the walker should flex the foot, ankle and lower calf muscles to propel the body forward. This push should continue until the toes of the supporting leg leave the ground. By rolling the foot off the ground, completely up to the toes, the walker is able to exert maximum forward propulsion and push throughout the stride.

As the foot leaves the ground, the push should originate from the second through the fifth toes. Pushing off from the big toe may cause inward hyperextension of the knee, resulting in loss of power and possible knee injury.

The driving leg should swing through directly under the hip in order to avoid *circumduction* and kicking the lower leg out to the side. Walkers should also avoid a high back-kick, an action which often leads to lifting.

Walkers must develop correct foot placement as part of their technique. In order to maximize stride length and power, the inside of each foot should land on the same straight line of the road or track. Walking on this straight line, as opposed to "marching" with feet apart, adds extra centimeters to each stride. Proper hip rotation also will result in this "straight line" foot placement.

Walking with the toes splaying outwards or pointing inwards leads to a loss of efficient stride length and makes it difficult to push forward when the foot reaches a flat position. The incorrect push that results will direct the body laterally, instead of straight ahead.

The Correction of Technique Faults

Without access to good technique coaching, many walkers must train themselves. These athletes must find methods for improvement on their own, such as videotapes and helpful advice, even if this means relying on relatively uninformed teammates, parents or friends to watch for telltale indicators of technique faults. Walkers usually do not learn that they have a technique problem until they receive disqualification calls from the judges. Many times athletes discover their technique faults only as the problem begins to cause an injury.

Because of this general lack of useful technique information, walkers must take every opportunity to work with a knowledgeable technique coach whenever and wherever they find one. Athletes should demand that these resource people offer *solutions* to technique problems, instead of merely identifying the particular fault.

Once walkers identify their technique faults and learn the solutions, they must begin a remedial routine to reform the incorrect technique permanently. How long will it take to correct a specific problem using such routines? Even in the best conditions, results may not come quickly. The accepted rule is to allow a minimum of three months, and a maximum of six months, to establish a major technique change. However, the period of time that a walker has spent using faulty technique is the main factor in determining the exact recovery time. Because bad technique habits are self-perpetuating, it is essential for walkers to seek out solutions immediately when a problem is detected.

The solution, whether an exercise routine, style change or some other regimen, must be followed faithfully even at the expense of other conditioning. Although exercises are usually boring and style changes may result in slower times at first, the end result— faster times, fewer injuries and no disqualifications— are certainly worth the work.

Changes must be made gradually, especially if a style problem has existed for a long period of time. Because previously unused and weak muscles come into play, walkers who try to make instant and complete changes while they continue to train may create other problems for themselves. A moderate, controlled approach can be more effective; for instance, during a training spin use the new technique for about one minute, and then revert to your old method for five minutes. As you increase in strength, the periods using the new technique can become longer. This alternating between old and improved techniques will also increase your awareness of the differences between the two styles.

Following are several common technique faults and effective solutions that I have encountered during my years as a competitor and coach. Not all of these faults automatically lead to disqualification and/or injury, but they at least contribute to fatigue. Although other exercises, medical treatments and strength building routines may exist, the following presentation highlights the classic race walking problems and problem areas, and gives the most proven methods of overcoming them.

Developing Correct Posture

Body Lean

Whether a walker is leaning too far forward or back, the problems which result are the same— tight upper body, a raise in the body's center of gravity and probable disqualifications. The solutions to these problems are also similar. If you detect such faults in your own technique, try the following disciplines:

- Walk at a slow pace, first leaning forward, and then backward. Notice how the body sensations differ in each position. You will observe a definite push or driving feeling when leaning forward and a "reaching out" with the driving leg when leaning

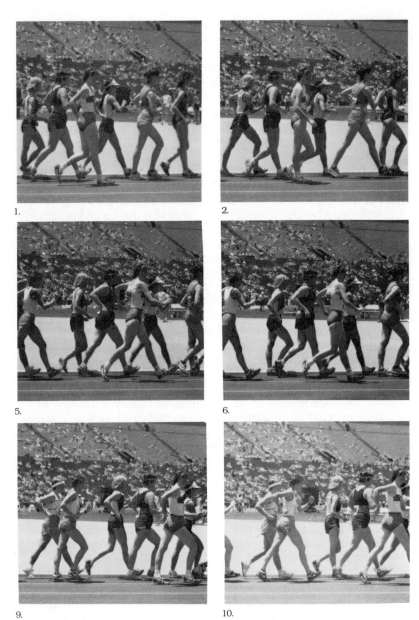

1.   2.

5.   6.

9.   10.

*The 1984 Women's 10,000 meter exhibition walk during the
Olympic trials reveals a diversion of techniques. Notice the
various body leans and ranges of arm motion in particular; most
of the actions shown are examples of inefficient technique.*
(Photos by Tom Carroll.)

3.   4.

7.   8.

11.   12.

backwards. Strive for the push sensation.
- The optimum 5° angle of lean can be developed in the following manner: Stand relaxed with your feet shoulder-length apart. Now lean forward *from the heel* until you need to step forward to keep from falling. Try race walking holding this same angle of lean.
- Because walking with a strong forward lean places extra stress on the Achilles tendon and ankle joint, strength and mobility in these areas must be developed. Specific stretching routines for such improvement are found in chapter 6.
- Eliminating any swayback tendencies (see below) will help keep the hips from dropping behind the waist. "Walk tall," avoiding any tendency to curve the upper back and roll the shoulders forward. The shoulder exercise on page 46 is excellent for eliminating this fault.
- Watch for any signs of poor body posture and incorrect lean, such as, an "s" curve of the back, which indicates rib cage dropping behind waist; or the waistband of the shorts angling down from back to front, which indicates swayback.

Swayback

A common condition among wakers is *swayback*, a posture problem caused by weak lower abdominal muscles and a tight lower back. Swayback, which is a visible inward curve of the lower spine, probably causes more technique problems than any other posture condition since it makes proper vertical and horizontal hip action virtually impossible to attain.

Correcting swayback by strengthening the lower abdominal muscles and increasing lower back flexibility should be the primary training goal of any walker who has this condition. Stretching and mobility exercises, which will help develop lower back flexibility, can also be found in chapter 6. In addition, the following set of exercises recommended by Kinesiologist Karen Clippinger-Robertson, are excellent for strengthening the lower abdominal muscles. Sit-ups, the method usually prescribed to strengthen stomach muscles, may actually do more harm than good; most forms of sit-ups strengthen the hip flexor muscles and tighten lower back muscles, resulting in even greater forward pressure on the lower spine.

- Pelvic Tilt—A basic and simple exercise, the pelvic tilt is an effective way to warm up the lower abdominals and practice the correct muscle isolation for later exercises. Lying flat on the back, flatten the area immediately below the belt line and keep it pressed against the floor for 10-15 seconds, repeating 7-10 times. Be sure to keep the upper back flat and to pull in the lower abdominal wall, especially the oblique muscles.
- Curl-Up—Maintaining the pelvic tilt and bending the knees, slowly curl up until the shoulder blades are well off the ground. Hold this position for 10-15 seconds for each of 7-10 repetitions. Be sure to keep the lower abdominal muscles tucked in throughout each repetition of the exercise.

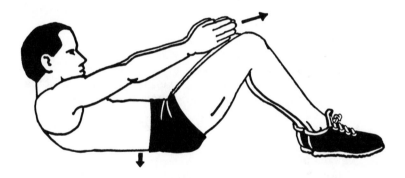

- Curl-Up with Rotation—In the curl-up position, twist the upper body to one side, hold for 10-15 seconds and curl back to the floor. Now curl up and twist to the other side, again holding 10-15 seconds. Repeat the full exercise 7-10 times. Be sure to maintain the pelvic tilt position with the abdominal wall tucked in, and keep each hip squarely on the ground.

Improving Shoulder and Upper Torso Action

As discussed earlier, rigid shoulders and tight upper torso muscles limit hip extension and cause other style problems as well. A short, inefficient stride and danger of lifting result. Because tension is a major factor in causing tight shoulders, relieving daily stress during serious race walking training periods is critical to your athletic performance. There are, however, more practical solutions for improving shoulder and upper torso action:

- Whenever doing push-ups and other weight work, concentrate on keeping a flat back. Avoid the natural tendency to let the shoulder blades come together and fully extend your arms when pushing up the weight.
- Be sure that you are using arm action within the proper range of motion.
- Develop the feeling of extending the shoulder muscles under the armpit—the lower trapezius and the latissimus dorsi in particular—while swinging the arm forward and backward.
- Avoid excessive vertical rotation of the shoulders. The shoulders should never raise higher than their normal position when completely relaxed.
- Think of the spine as a stationary rod, with the body rotating around it. The torso should not sway from side-to-side nor front-to-back.
- Keep the forearms and elbows low when bringing the arms forward past the waistband. The thumb and elbow should remain in line with the waistband when swinging past it. This action helps keep the shoulders low and moving through the correct range of motion.
- Concentrate on the mobility exercises described in chapter 6.

Improving Arm Action

Walkers must learn to recognize the indicators of good arm action, as outlined in the preceding section, "The Elements of Race Walking Technique." To review: Keep your hands loosely clenched; swing the hands and elbows through low at waistband level; drive the elbow of the rear arm back aggressively, but not up, while keeping the shoulder low; always return the hands to the same spot in front of the body—nipple-high and about six inches in front of the chest; and avoid excessive lateral movement with the elbows as they drive back.

You will develop a correct arm swing and drive by developing good shoulder and torso action as described above and by striving to work in the ideal range of motion. Practice the following exercises and disciplines:

- Walk in place in front of a mirror and check to see if your arms and shoulders are covering the proper range of motion. As suggested earlier, wearing a white shirt marked with a "t" when performing this discipline will help in developing the proper action.

Some of the world's leading women race walkers display excessive lateral arm and hip motion during the 1983 Eschborn Cup. Australia's Sue Cook leads here. (Photo by Wayne Glusker.)

- Do not push up with the hands when they are in front of the body or with the elbows in back. Exert relaxed power and push only as the arms drive forward and backward along the waistband area.
- To develop proper arm action in front of the body, have someone run next to you while you walk, holding their hand six inches in front of your chest at nipple level. Your hands should swing up strongly to the point as high as their hand and no higher.

Improving Hip Action

Beginning walkers, especially those who have pursued another sport seriously in the past, often have inflexible hips, and consequently achieve little forward extension. To check for horizontal rotation, observe the stripe on the side of a walker's shorts. When he or she is standing still, these stripes should be in line with the vertical carriage of the body. While the athlete is walking, the stripes should move forward as well as in back of this vertical line of the body.

Walking legally at high speed without proper vertical and horizontal hip action is almost impossible. To develop proper hip rotation and extension, practice these disciplines:

- Walk with the inside of each foot landing on the same straight line.
- Be sure to develop the complete ideal range of motion of your arm swing. The hips will follow this motion, as the forward swinging phase of the arm brings about greater forward extension of the opposite hip and vice versa.
- Holding the body in the swayback position is perhaps the most common cause of poor hip extension. Refer to "Developing Correct Posture" above for methods to overcome this condition.
- Incorporate the mobility exercises, described in chapter 6, into your daily routine.
- Develop the sensation of pushing forward and down with the bottom of each buttock when swinging the advancing leg through.

Some race walkers, both deliberately and unintentionally, have developed a technique of using a high hip drive, which causes almost all of the vertical hip rotation to disappear. While this technique can be effective in creating a fast strike rate, it also results in bringing the driving foot through high with a back-kick of the rear foot. As previously discussed, the high hip drive places a great deal of percussive stress on the ankle and knee joints, and may lead to chronic injuries. Allowing the hip to roll down vertically as it drives forward horizontally is the better method.

Upper body tension, especially when the shoulders roll and lift or hunch forward, also contributes to this high hip drive action. As is the case with many technique problems, developing proper shoulder action is one of the first steps that should be taken to develop proper hip rotation.

This walker is exhibiting an extreme soft-knee technique, barely straightening enough to fulfill the rules of legality. Note the tensed quadracep and the premature flattening of the supporting foot, neither of which contribute to fast times. (Photo by Wayne Glusker.)

Improving Knee Action

Unless it is done intentionally to rest the hamstrings or to gain speed by pushing with the quadracep muscles, walking with the knees illegally bent in the vertical support position— or creeping— results from overall weakness, lack of general flexibility or attempting to utilize a running motion using incorrect arm and hip action. Use the following measures in your efforts to overcome creeping:

- Increase the flexibility of the calves and hamstring muscles.
- Warm up thoroughly, especially before a speed session.
- Emphasize the high forefoot action when the heel strikes the ground. This action helps to straighten the knee by extending the lower leg slightly.
- Increase the static stretching ability of the area immediately behind the knee.

In your attempts to improve knee straightening, remember not to strive for a locked knee position. A straightening action that will meet the demands of judging is all that is necessary.

Improving Foot and Ankle Action

Technique problems with the foot and ankle area, such as feet flattening prematurely, "toeing-out" and "toeing-in," or pushing off the driving foot before it rolls up on the toes, may not result in disqualification, but will rob a walker of vital power and stride length. Whatever the

1.

2.

3.

4.

5.

6.

American Walkers Tim Lewis (left) and Vince O'Sullivan (right) demonstrate relaxed walking styles during the 1984 Olympic trials. Notice Lewis' extreme rear knee extension, a technique which gives him considerable forward propulsive power, when coupled with leg strength. A walker with less leg strength, such as O' Sullivan, benefits more from bending the rear knee sooner. (Photos by Tom Carroll.)

problem, building overall strength and flexibility of the
ankle joint and feet is the first solution.

The following exercises have proven very effective in
improving foot and ankle action:

- Use your hand to twist the foot in small circles
  through its entire range of motion, performing this
  exercise 5-6 times with each foot.
- Write the alphabet in the air with the big toe to the
  point of joint exhaustion.
- Hang a small weight (approximately 2 lbs. to start)
  from the forefoot and sit on a bench or counter. Lift
  the weight with the toes through a full vertical and
  lateral range of motion. Begin with 2-3 sets of 10
  repetitions.

Poor foot placement and action often reflects a lack of
good technique in other areas. For instance, driving the
hips through too high with excessive knee flexion lifts the
foot and causes a high back-kick; leaning too far forward
causes the forefoot to flatten prematurely, before the foot
passes under the body's center; and failure to bring the
hands up to the nipple level during the drive phase prevents
the walker from landing with a high forefoot. Because of
these correlations, walkers can often improve foot action
by following the suggested corrective routines for such
problems in other areas.

Possibly the most career-endangering condition a
walker can develop involves circumduction of the foot and
the knee. In the most classic case the walker whips the
front of the driving foot out to the side, with the knee
hyperextending inwards. This action places great pressure
on the knee and ankle joints, and limits forward
propulsion as well.

To correct this condition, practice the ankle and foot
exercises given above. While walking, keep the knee of the
supporting leg slightly to the outside of the supporting foot
at all times (slightly bowlegged, as opposed to knock-
kneed). In addition, practice driving off the second through
the fifth toes of the supporting foot, instead of the big toe.
Circumduction is often due to muscle imbalances which
can be detected and treated with proper exercises by a
sports therapist.

Summary

Most walkers have at least one area of technique
which requires improvement and many athletes have

several technique faults. If you fall into the latter category, the following priority list will help you to plan which areas to attack first in your improvement training:

1. Circumduction of the driving leg
2. Swayback; weak lower abdominals
3. Weak or inefficient arm carriage
4. Tight upper body, shoulders and torso
5. Excessive lateral motion of the hips, torso and/or arms

As stated earlier, correcting one of these areas will almost always result in a corresponding improvement in other elements of technique.

The preceding pages may seem to portray race walking as the most technical event in athletics and incredibly difficult to perfect, but this is definitely not the case. Rather, the fact that technique can almost always be improved reflects an enormous amount of potential gain for the serious competitor. Virtually every race walking technique improvement results in greater speed with less effort, less chance of injury and a smoother race with less risk of disqualification.

A competitor who has excellent technique and good training habits, but still is not getting the desired results, is the athlete who has the most serious problem. The competitor who is already performing well, but still needs additional improvement in technique, should be the most optimistic; this athlete can make enormous gains by devoting just a small amount of training time each day to technique improvement.

Chapter V

Training for Endurance

After technique, endurance training offers the greatest potential for improvement. Strength and speed can be increased only to a limited extent, but endurance can be increased dramatically by correct training. Building stamina also requires more training time than strength or speed improvements. Even though technique improvement is even more important, endurance training is more time-consuming and will take up the bulk of the available training time.

Endurance in this sport must be defined as the ability to hold a rapid tempo for a significant period of time; competitive race walking is a speed event even at the 50 kilometer distance. Improvement in this area is brought about by improving the body's ability to supply fuel (in the form of glycogen) and oxygen to the muscles.

Training to Build the Body's Oxygen Supply

Because the lungs are responsible for bringing oxygen to the bloodstream, developing greater capacity of these organs is one of the keys for building stamina. Athletes must seriously concentrate on the way they breathe in order to use the full potential of the lungs. An athlete takes the maximum amount of oxygen into the lungs by *belly breathing*, which requires breathing with the sternum area immediately below the diaphragm, as well as with the chest cavity. Deep breathing in training, exhaling completely and resisting the urge to "pant" are the most effective methods for opening the diaphragm and developing belly breathing.

From the lungs, oxygen is transferred to the bloodstream and pumped to the muscles by the heart. Therefore, a stronger heart with greater pumping capacity is also vital to increasing endurance. In order to improve its performance, the heart must be exercised using the same principles as any other muscle. The most beneficial way to exercise muscles for endurance is by training in the *aerobic/anaerobic threshold.*

In the aerobic state (on the average, below 130 heart beats per minute), the body's muscles are continually supplied with oxygen and function in only a mildly stressed state. In the anaerobic state (more than 150 beats per minute), the muscles are not receiving enough oxygen and fatigue rapidly sets in.

The aerobic/anaerobic threshold lies between these levels of exertion, when the heart is working between 130 and 150 beats per minute. In this threshold range, all muscles, including the heart, are being stressed to a degree that properly promotes maximum adaptation.

Because the red blood cells, which are pumped to the muscles by the heart, carry oxygen, the body must have an adequate supply. Red blood cells are actually destroyed in training, particularly in a sport such as race walking, where the feet pound the ground continually and many muscle groups are severely taxed. Due to this effect, a walker's red blood cell count may decrease when a new level of training intensity is initiated. However, given proper rest and adequate nutrition, the body quickly builds the count back up to its original level. As the body adapts to the continued stress of training, the red blood cell count continues to increase. The walker is now able to train harder without the resulting fatigue and slow adaptation caused by a low supply of red blood cells.

The capillary network is the final link between the heart and muscle tissue, and is the point where fuel and oxygen actually enter the muscle tissue. Increasing capillary capacity is vital to improving endurance, and race walkers should develop this capacity specific to the muscles most often used in race walking.

As a muscle, joint or tissue area is exercised more and more, the surrounding capillary network compensates by expanding to supply the area with more blood. Continuous exercise rather than sudden bursts— or steady endurance walking in the aerobic state rather than intervals— best achieves this vital process. Too many anaerobic sessions, such as hard intervals and excessive time trials (for the typical athlete, more than two such sessions per week), break down the capillary networks beyond their capacity for quick healing and progressive adaptation.

This emphasis on capillary development explains why race walkers are in better overall condition than runners who may be following a similar training program; because walking uses more of the body's total muscular system, more capillary networks are enlarged.

One goal of endurance training must be to raise the anaerobic threshold level and thereby increase the amount of work that a walker can perform during the aerobic state. The higher the threshold, the less energy the walker will expend at a certain pace.

The best way to raise the threshold is to train in long intervals of 20 to 30 minutes in duration at a tempo near target race pace. Five thousand meters is an ideal interval distance for threshold training, with a target tempo of the current 10,000 meter race pace. More detailed information about threshold workouts is presented in chapter 9.

Training to Build the Body's Glycogen Supply

Glucose, along with oxygen, is carried by the bloodstream to the muscles, giving them their energy. Glucose is stored as *glycogen* in the muscles and liver, and literally serves as the body's fuel supply.

When training begins, the small amount of glucose that is stored in the blood stream is spent quickly, and the body begins converting glycogen to glucose and speeding it to the muscles. During this complex process, *lactic acid* is produced as a by-product. As training continues, lactic acid begins to accumulate as waste. Although a small amount is released through perspiration and exhalation, any accumulation of lactic acid causes muscular discomfort.

Glycogen levels continue to drop during lengthy training periods and the body produces more lactic acid wastes. In high speed training, the body cannot burn an adequate supply of glycogen, fats or proteins for energy, and so quickly runs out of fuel. In medium speed training, the body maintains an adequate supply of glycogen for approximately 90 minutes. In distance-aerobic training, glycogen is depleted more gradually, and the body usually maintains a sufficient amount of this fuel for at least 30 kilometers.

The body's glycogen supply is built up through *depletion training*, in which an athlete first depletes glycogen through a long, exhausting walk, and then replenishes the supply with rest and a high-carbohydrate diet. These long walks are not intended to move the body into an anaerobic state, and in fact, should be performed just below the aerobic/anaerobic threshold. The exercise should produce muscle tightness and fatigue, not cardiovascular exhaustion.

With the above facts in mind, it is fairly easy to answer the question of how much distance work to perform and how long the sessions should be. Twenty kilometer specialists need not work into the stages of complete glycogen depletion. However, they do need to build vascular strength through medium distance workouts, reaching 30 kilometers during one weekly training spin. Fifty kilometer walkers should completely deplete themselves by walking well over 35 kilometers in one session at least once per month, and up to 35 kilometers per session once per week. If such depletion walks are attempted very early in a training program, the body will become too exhausted to adapt quickly.

The distance of workouts must be increased gradually; for example, walkers should increase from two-hour to four-hour walks over a period of several months, rather than making such a change immediately.

Chapter VI

Training for Speed

Once an endurance base has been established, improving speed should be the next task that is undertaken in a goal-oriented training plan. Before incorporating speed training into a workout schedule, it is extremely important for walkers and their coaches to understand certain physiological factors which will be affected by this change.

Oxygen Supply

When stressed to the maximum by short-distance walks at very high speed, the body will reach its limit in the maximum amount of oxygen which it can burn. This limit, known as the VO_2 *Max*, is reached at the greatest levels of exertion and determines the amount of time an athlete can sustain his or her top speed. The higher an athlete's VO_2 max, the greater the race walking potential. A walker can improve VO_2 max with anaerobic speed training and by trimming away excess pounds which subtract from VO_2 max potential.

Glycogen Supply

When athletes walk at their highest speeds, they are walking beyond the aerobic/anaerobic threshold, or in other words, working anaerobically. This phase will not occur in distance training, because the pulse rate remains in or below the threshold.

During the anaerobic phase, the walker will rapidly use the glucose stored in the muscles and much of the readily available supply of glycogen in the liver. As discussed earlier in chapter 5 on endurance training, energy is then produced by a complicated series of chemical reactions among the body's reserves, during which time a considerable amount of lactic acid forms. This process creates lactacid energy, explaining why another term for the anaerobic stage is the *lactacid stage.*

Because of the pain created by lactacid work, a walker cannot rely on this energy for long periods of time and should not do so to any extent. The body's reserves are drained quickly during the lactacid stage and overstress can easily result. Illness and injury follow too many prolonged sessions of lactacid training, or a hard, anaerobic race for which the body has not been sufficiently prepared.

Some anaerobic workouts should be maintained year-round to avoid the need to increase VO_2 max and make necessary technique adjustments for attaining speed all at once. But because prime lactacid strength can only be sustained for two or three months, concentrated speed training should occur only in the last few weeks approaching the most important racing season.

Aerobic and Anaerobic Ranges, VO_2 Max, and Heart Beat Rate of a Race Walker in Good Condition

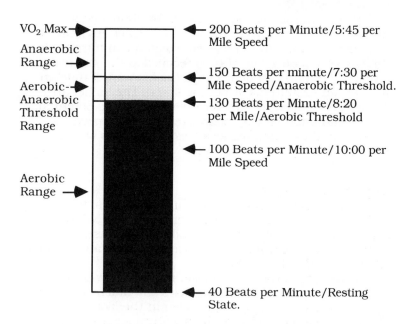

Improving Race Walking Speed

Because race walking speed must be attained and maintained *legally*, speed alone will not win walking races. However, there is no doubt that superior speed, whether natural or developed, plays a major part in successful race walking just as it does in any other sport.

Even a 50 kilometer walker cannot neglect speed; in order to average 24:00 for each 5,000 meter leg of a 50 kilometer race (maintaining a four-hour pace), the athlete must be able to walk 5,000 meters alone in at least 21:00. Any slower, and the walker will be working too near his or her VO_2 max in the attempt to maintain a 24:00 pace per 5,000 meters, and will soon reach the exhausting anaerobic state.

While it is well known that a preponderance of *fast-twitch muscle* tissue is necessary for natural speed, race walking offers more hope than most sports to those athletes burdened with excessive "slow twitchers;" the naturally fast walkers must be able to use their higher percentage of fast-twitch muscles *legally*.

Depending upon the walker's level of conditioning, the body tends toward several danger points in high-speed walking: upper body tension increases; the arms reach higher in front and in back; and the stride shortens—all possibly leading to a lifting violation and disqualification. A walker can avoid this loss of control by keeping the arms low, working them harder past the waistband area in a forward-and-backward action rather than thrusting up and down with the elbows and hands. While controlling the arm action, the walker can maintain stride length by emphasizing the forward thrust of the supporting leg just as the foot is about to leave the ground.

Assuming that speed technique and the fast-twitch/slow-twitch muscle ratio are roughly equal between two walkers, what can one do to build leg speed and increase the strength to hold it?

Improve VO_2 Max. A walker can improve VO_2 max to an extent with specific interval training, working at speeds near the present VO_2 max. This type of training should add up to no more than 10 percent of the total weekly mileage. These interval workouts should consist of hard efforts between four and seven minutes each. Rest periods between the efforts should be shorter than the time of the effort itself. More specifics on how to plan and coordinate VO_2 workouts in an individual training schedule are given later in the introduction to chapter 9. A walker can also improve VO_2 max by eliminating excess fatty tissue.

Improve Economy. If a walker has technique
problems or lacks the strength for speed walking, these
weaknesses will become more apparent while he or she is
working in the lactacid state. The walker with less
proficient technique and/or less strength will need more
energy to sustain a similar speed, thus creating more
lactacids than the walker with the better technique or more
strength. In addition to following the tips given in the
preceding chapters on improving basic technique, specific
economy workouts can be added to a training schedule
which improve speed technique and strength. These
workout are based on the principles of stress and
compensation; by working the body above its limits of
efficient technique and present conditioning, it will adapt to
higher levels of stress. Supplementary technique exercises
must be performed at the same time to help achieve this
more efficient style.

Economy workouts are similar to VO_2 max workouts,
but are faster and cover shorter distances. Also, the rest
periods between hard efforts must be longer then the time
of the actual workout efforts. Economy workouts should
make up no more than 6 percent of total weekly mileage.
Specifics on incorporating economy workouts into a
training program are also given later in the introduction to
chapter 9.

In addition to the more regulated methods of speed
training discussed above, walkers can take the following,
less precise measures to improve speed and the strength to
maintain it:

- Increase flexibility. Tightness in muscles and joints
  will shorten as well as slow the walker's stride.
  Because speed training actually *tightens* muscles, it
  is doubly important to emphasize flexibility routines
  while engaged in the speed work phases of a
  training program.
- Build strength and power in speed-producing
  muscle groups. Technique-specific strength work as
  described in chapter 8, helps the walker to achieve
  the muscular strength to produce maximum speed
  and rebound tendency from the propulsive phase,
  and increase the strike rate.
- Practice walking down hills at fast tempo. Taking
  150-200 meter spins down 5° black top roads (a
  concrete surface is too hard) at faster-than-race-

pace is an excellent method for achieving a high strike rate without a major amount of strain.
Because this exercise allows the walker to achieve fast speeds with minimum effort, it serves as a good final tune-up before a major race.
- Work on a motorized treadmill. Gradually increasing the speed while walking on a motorized treadmill will help develop leg speed. The controlled environment also allows walkers to remain relaxed while they build speed.
- Get pacing help from a faster walker or runner. Concentrating on someone walking immediately ahead, especially during track workouts, often can pull walkers along at a faster tempo than they would achieve on their own.
- Be certain to warm up well before speed training and racing sessions. Muscles should be loose and the heart rate elevated prior to the actual workout, or it will be difficult to achieve fast times and strong speed technique. A typical warm-up might consist of 2 miles of easy strolling, followed by 8-10 hard 100 meter efforts.

Summary

VO$_2$ max, the maximum amount of oxygen an athlete can burn when under maximum stress, is a major factor in determining an athlete's potential. One of the most important goals in speed training should be to raise the VO$_2$ max, working at this rate or near it for a designated period of time. Athletes with a high VO$_2$ max, but lacking the conditioning to work near this rate for a sufficient length of time, will be out-walked by lower-max athletes who have a superior training background and the strength to work closer to their maximum oxygen burning level.

If you are somewhat confused by the elements of speed training, there is good reason. Juggling the amount of speed-versus-slower training, knowing the amount of anaerobic work which can be tolerated and recognizing when a walker is losing technique as a result of speed work— these are the elements which embody the complex and challenging training questions of our sport. There are not, and may never be, exact formulas to answer such questions. Walkers and their coaches must strive to find the training formulas that work best for them. The training tables in chapter 9 are an excellent starting point.

Chapter VII

Training for Flexibility

Almost all athletes and coaches, whatever their sport, agree on the importance of flexibility and relaxation. Both capacities are of particular importance in race walking. Because so many parts of the body come into play in this sport, tightness and rigidity anywhere will affect speed, power and legality.

Many people think of themselves as flexible if they can perform some popular test of flexibility— touching their toes without bending the knees, for example. However, even a very tight person may be able to demonstrate a degree of *static flexibility* by performing a certain stretching routine. Successful race walking demands *dynamic flexibility*, a combination of static flexibility, mobility and relaxation throughout a wide range of motion.

Although race walking uses a wider range of motion than running, for instance, walking still involves repetitions over certain controlled ranges of motion. These movements in themselves do little to improve flexibility. Furthermore, working the same muscles repetitively in any range of motion actually creates shorter muscles. For these reasons, supplemental flexibility exercises are especially valuable.

Common areas of low flexibility in race walkers include the hamstrings, calves, the lower back and front shoulder muscles. In the worst case, this tightness can lead to injuries, or at least decreased performances. For example, a typical consequence of tight calf muscles is *pronation*, a condition which allows more range of motion at the ankle but contributes to shin splints, Achilles tendonitis and other lower extremity problems.

Tight lower back musculature often contributes to swayback, causing a range of problems in a race walker's technique— the failure to bring the pelvis under when driving forward with the hip, high hip carriage and a loss of power and stride length. Increasing dynamic flexibility in any of these areas can be accomplished by performing mobility exercises and/or strength training using a full range of motion. Various methods of stretching described below are also effective.

Methods of Stretching

Static Stretching

Static stretching exercises require an athlete to hold a position that places a particular muscle or muscle group and related connective tissue in a near fully-lengthened position. This position should be held for 30 seconds to one minute. A slow, gentle stretch is recommended, with an effort to relax the muscle and to let it lengthen. If properly performed, static stretching provides both a safe and effective way of increasing flexibility.

Ballistic Stretching

Ballistic stretching involves bouncy movements, such as quick, repetitive toe touches. This technique creates some concern among coaches and sports trainers because the quick stretch causes a quick reflex contraction of the muscle being stretched, with accompanying pain and risk of injury. Ballistic stretching routines are not recommended.

PNF Techniques

Proprioceptive Neuromuscular Facilitation (PNF) Techniques are the most recent stretching method to come into use for athletes. These techniques, which alternate stretching with muscle contractions, are used to alter the nervous system's influence on the muscle in order to gain more flexibility, and are particularly useful for stretching muscle groups that do not respond well to static stretching.

One example of PNF stretching is a 10-second contraction of the muscle, followed by a 10-second stretch. This pattern is repeated three times and then followed with a 30-second static stretch.

General Stretching Guidelines

Both static and PNF stretching routines are best performed when the muscles are warm and connective joints are flexible. Avoid stretching in the morning; the best stretching times are before an afternoon workout or later in the evening. Whatever technique is used, walkers should stretch three or four times per week, and high mileage walkers need stretching every day, since their training calls for many repetitive movements over a limited range of motion.

A stretching routine should include one to three repetitions per muscle group with a sustained hold of 30 seconds or longer. Be sure to stretch each side of the body equally in order to develop symmetry between the right and left sides. Practice relaxing when stretching by breathing evenly (do not hold your breath), avoiding pain, and "letting tension go" throughout the *entire* body.

Static Flexibility Routine for Race Walkers

The following static and PNF stretches are presented in a natural order for routines and one exercise flows easily to the next. Literally hundreds of other stretching routines exist. Indeed, entire books have been written on stretching alone. Yet, in my own experience, most athletes do as little stretching as possible. In order to be realistic, only a small number of routines are described here. The following routine, contributed by Kinesiologist Karen Clippinger-Robertson, represents the most important stretches for race walkers and should be incorporated into every serious walker's training program.

- *Hamstring Stretch*— Isolate one leg at a time, with the other tucked in, making sure to keep the hips square. Keep the weight of the upper body in front of the hip socket, bending the knee if necessary.

• *Hip Adductor Stretch*— Pull in the abdominal wall. Emphasize leaning forward from the hip sockets.

• *Hip Abductor Stretch*— Keep both hips down, bringing one knee at a time over the other leg and across the body.

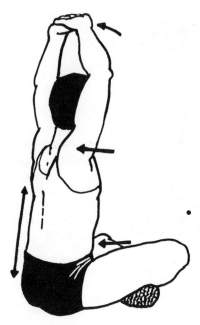

- *Shoulder Extensors and Internal Rotators Stretch—* Pull the arms and shoulders back, keeping the lower back straight and shoulders low.

- *Lower Back Stretch—* Hold the lower back flat against the floor. Pull the knees to the chest using the abdominals. Keep the head on the floor and the neck stretched long. This stretch is especially good for overcoming swayback.

- *Quadriceps Stretch*— Keeping the lower back flat, pull the leg back with the lower leg in line with the thigh. Decrease pressure if knee pain occurs.

- *Hip Flexor Stretch*— Keeping the lower back flat, bring the bottom of the pelvis under and forward, one side at a time. This stretch is another important method for overcoming swayback.

- *Calf (Gastrocnemius) Stretch—* Keeping the lower back flat and both feet parallel, lean forward with straight legs. Keep the heel on the floor. It is best not to lean against a wall when performing this exercise.

- *Calf (Soleus) Stretch—* Keeping the lower back flat, feet parallel, and knees over the toes, lean forward. Keep the heel on the floor.

Dynamic Flexibility Routines for Race Walkers

The following exercises have been developed specifically for race walkers' use. They are designed to increase dynamic flexibility by increasing mobility and the range of motion of the muscle and connective tissue groups most important to good race walking technique.

Although each of the exercises is designed to improve race walking action in certain areas of the body, such as the shoulders or hips, they have been presented here rather than in "The Correction of Technique Faults" (chapter 4) for good reason: these exercises work together and should be performed as a set. For maximum benefit, the routines should also be combined with static stretching exercises and relaxation techniques.

Walkers should incorporate these dynamic flexibility exercises into every warm-up, particularly before a race, and will also find it useful to work through these routines during a long distance workout to prevent muscle tightness. Each routine should be performed while race walking at a pace of approximately 9:30 per mile.

As with all exercises, relaxation and regular breathing are important factors for deriving the most benefit from the following routines.

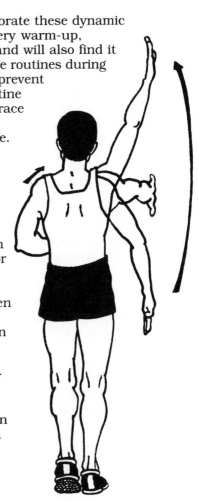

- *Windmill*— This is an excellent exercise for shoulder flexibility and developing the coordination between shoulders and hips. While walking, begin swinging the right arm completely around the shoulder clockwise, keeping the elbow straight. This action will open up the shoulder area by forcing the swinging shoulder back and the other forward. After performing the desired number of revolutions with the right arm, switch to the left arm. Now work both arms. Be sure to keep the feet landing in a straight line to insure proper hip rotation and maintain a pelvic tilt. Starting with 20 revolutions with each arm, and 40 with both arms, work up to 50 revolutions with each arm, 80-100 with both.

- *Cross-Over*— To increase hip flexibility while walking, clasp hands chest-high and exaggerate forward hip extension, crossing the feet over a straight line. Let the arms swing freely across the body keeping the hands clasped and elbows bent at a 90° angle. Practice the cross-over for 100-150 strides.
- *Shoulder Roll*— To reduce shoulder tension while walking, exaggerate the shoulder roll and concentrate on making large vertical ovals with the tips of the shoulders. Keep the arms relaxed. Practice this movement for 70-100 strides.
- *Hands Behind Body*— For building overall shoulder-hip coordination, grasp hands behind body with the elbows at a 90° angle. Let the shoulders and hips relax completely as you walk in this position. Maintain the exercise for 70-100 strides.
- *Uphill Hip Walk*— To build hip power and extension, hold a small ball (approximately the size of a softball) in front of you shoulder-high. Now walk up a slight hill at rapid tempo, keeping the ball steady both laterally and vertically. This exercise will force the hips to do most of the work. Repeat the routine throughout several 50 meter intervals.

Walkers can practice these sets of exercises to the point of exhaustion and sore muscles if the remainder of the workout is fairly light. If these exercises are used as part of a race warm-up, walkers should perform the minimum number needed to feel coordinated and relaxed.

Relaxation

Proper relaxation allows walkers to translate increased flexibility and mobility into good race walking technique. If walkers cannot leave tensions behind them when beginning a workout or race, the body simply will not relax, making it difficult for different areas to work together in strong, flowing, coordinated movements.

Outside help may be necessary to help a walker "tune out" the pressures of daily life. Such disciplines as aikido or hatha yoga have been shown to improve both physical and mental relaxation. Sports psychiatrists have also aided many walkers in overcoming the inability to relax. Becoming a "walking bum"— unemployed and generally avoiding the pressures of living in twentieth century America— has proven effective for some walkers, but this, of course, is not a practical, long-range solution.

Even without outside help, a walker can often improve relaxation skills by consciously practicing ways to reduce tension while training. Avoid upper body tension, for instance, by keeping the face relaxed and the shoulders loose. This rule is particularly important to remember during speed work and the finish of hard training sessions.

Chapter VIII

Training for Strength

If a walker is attempting to overcome specific technique problems or injuries with strength-building routines, time *must* be taken away from other training to allow for these routines. The amount of time which should be devoted to *general* strength-building routines, however, is a question still open to debate. This chapter concentrates on general strength building training.

We do not know how much time the world's best walkers spend on general strength building routines. Even without a consensus, logic alone dictates that when all else is equal, the walker with the most powerful physique must dominate. Stronger muscles simply can maintain speed for a longer period of time.

If training time permits, walkers are well-advised to add general strength building routines to their programs; these routines, however, should never interfere with more important training for technique, endurance, speed and flexibility. When making this adjustment, four types of routines are usually considered: weight training, isometrics, exercises and resistance walking. As the explanations below reveal, some of these methods are of more use to race walkers than others.

Weight Training

Working with weights is generally accepted to be the most effective way to increase muscular strength. Finding facilities for weight lifting is fairly simple, given the number of health and fitness clubs and the increased importance which university athletic departments invest in weight facilities.

Regardless of the types of weights used, whether free weights, nautilus equipment or others, there are several guidelines walkers should keep in mind.

- Three times per week is the suggested frequency for

weight workouts, twice weekly during the
competitive season.
* Lift light weights in high repetitions rather than
the reverse.
* Continually work to increase both the amount of
weight being lifted and the number of repetitions.
A good guildeline is to start with sets of 10
repetitions, and build to 20 before increasing the
weight. Don't worry about increases during the
competitive season.
* Be sure to cover a wide range of motion in all
routines and keep the muscles lengthened.
* Warm up well and keep warm during the entire
weight lifting session.

Isometrics
Isometric contractions build strength as force is
exerted against a stationary object, such as a fixed bar or
a wall. Isometrics are intended to increase explosive
power over a short distance, and so are of only limited use
for race walkers.

Exercises
Exercises do not in themselves force progressive
adaptation, and so are of best use in warming up and
warming down.

Resistance Walking
Resistance walking includes such routines as pulling
a weight while walking or wearing a weighted vest. The
obvious danger of such routines is that they force an
unnatural compensation and may bring the wrong
muscles into play.
New to race walking training are several methods
which have been used by progressive running coaches for
several years. These methods include ploymetrics,
bounding, and hill bounding. Any walker who has the
opportunity to work with a trainer experienced in any of
these routines should add them to his or her training
program as soon as possible. Each is aimed at increasing
the rebound tendency of the springing muscles, an action
that will produce considerable straight-ahead power when
coupled with good race walking technique.

Chapter IX

Training Schedules for Specific Racing Distances

The preceding chapters of *Advanced Race Walking* were written with the purpose of preparing the reader for the pages that follow— the actual day-to-day training schedules designed to help walkers reach their goals in the sport. These tables naturally assume that most walkers will undertake a demanding training schedule if they know the reasons behind it and the goals are worthwhile.

The training programs are aimed at helping an athlete reach peak form and condition for a particular racing season, when major trials and meets usually occur. For an American athlete, this racing season traditionally has encompassed a four-month period, beginning with a national race in early June, the Athletics Congress Nationals in mid-June, international dual meets in July and ending with the Lugano and Eschborn weekend, typically held in September. In the case of a junior athlete, the racing season could consist of the months of June and July, when the Age Group Nationals take place.

As mentioned earlier, the training principles and schedules presuppose that the reader is a serious, dedicated athlete...or at least willing to try to achieve this status. If you are less serious about the sport, simply scale down the intensity and length of the workouts proportionally to suit your own approach to race walking.

The Principles of a Training Program

1. The training program should be established with specific goals in mind.
2. The walker should gradually increase the mileage and/or intensity of his or her work load over the weeks, months and years.
3. The program primarily should emphasize endurance training.

4. The program should be based on cycles of difficult work followed by more moderate work.
5. Do not become a slave to a day-to-day training schedule.
6. A good warm-up and warm-down are essential and should always be included in the daily workout.
7. Always use correct and legal technique in training unless speed workouts specifically allow modification.
8. If you must alter your training schedule, always find time for the endurance workouts.

Principle One: *The training program should be established with specific goals in mind.* Decide on goals and consider the tasks which these goals might involve. The following ideas are just a sample of possible goals and the decisions they involve:

- *Make the Olympic team.* When should the training program begin, to allow optimum preparation for the Trials and the Games? What is your best distance— 20 or 50 kilometers? In what area— speed, endurance or technique— do you need the most outside assistance?
- *Be the top local walker.* This means maintaining roughly the same condition over the entire year. How often can you race and avoid injury? Should you focus on more major goals or is local competition enough, considering other factors?
- *Take 10 minutes off your 20 kilometer time.* Set a time frame in which to accomplish this goal. Will you achieve your target time by the end of the season or by a certain race? Do you need more speed or endurance in order to attain this time?
- *Eliminate a recurring disqualification problem.* What is the specific problem? What is the cause? Can you get a judge or experienced coach to work with you and eliminate the problem?

Principle Two: *The walker should gradually increase the mileage and/or intensity of the workload over the weeks, months and years.* It is impossible to advance from a local-level training schedule to a world-class program overnight. Despite the "guts," ability or natural strength you may have, the physiological makeup of the body still prevents such shortcuts. Expanded capillary networks, increased glycogen reserves and greater muscular strength can only be developed over time. If you do make a dramatic jump from a low to high-grade schedule, you will most likely suffer injuries, or at least deteriorate enough mentally and physically to wipe out early gains.

Principle Three: *The training program should primarily emphasize endurance training.* The graveyard of injured and forced-to-retire athletes is filled with walkers who failed to heed this advice and insisted on too much speed work too soon. It only takes a few weeks to reach nearly 100 percent of your speed potential, much longer to reach your endurance potential. But because speed workouts take less time and the results are more obvious, unguided walkers often overdo this type of training. Two potentially disastrous consequences may result: injury and the lack of a distance base during racing season.

Principle Four: *The training program should be based on cycles of difficult work followed by more moderate work.* The body must have time to adapt to progressively more strenuous workloads, as it develops more efficiency in processing wastes and greater capacity of capillary networks. This process cannot occur if the body is continually in an overstressed state. Although it is tempting to "pile on" hard workouts when improvement comes quickly, this tendency must be tempered with caution and faith in the overall training program.

Principle Five: *Do not become a slave to your training schedule.* In a perfect world, injuries, lack of motivation and distractions would never occur. This, of course, is not the case in the real world. Be positive and realistic about the training schedule you establish for yourself. Interruptions and bad days also affect your competitors. After a bad day or week, re-evaluate your schedule and pick up again as well as possible.

Principle Six: *A good warm-up and warm-down are absolutely essential and should always be included in the daily workout.* Good style is much easier to achieve when all of the body parts are warm and flexible. Incorporate into your warm-up any specific strength and flexibility exercises you are using to correct specific problems.

Principle Seven: *Always use correct and legal technique in training unless speed workouts specifically allow modifications.* Sloppy style practices at any time are counter-productive and reinforce bad habits. Maximize your workout time by constantly concentrating on correct technique. Because you must learn to sustain control in racing situations, it is particularly important to maintain good technique in training even when exhausted.

Principle Eight: *If you must alter your training schedule, always find time for endurance workouts.* If you must miss workouts, miss the speed workouts. Only one exception to this rule exists—when a major race is very near. Otherwise, you can concentrate on speed workouts later to overcome any setbacks; rebuilding a mileage base is much more difficult than improving leg speed.

The Yearly Plans

Four complete yearly training plans are presented in the following pages: a program for junior walkers and for those walkers concentrating on 10,000, 20,000 and 50,000 meter distances. Each plan is designed for walkers who intend to follow the preceding principles and aim at a particular season or race. Each program also requires a high level of dedication, perhaps more than the average reader is ready to assume. Although readers may modify the schedules if they feel it is necessary, all segments of the program must be changed proportionately. (For example, if you decrease the weekly mileage of workouts by half, cut back even more than half of your speed work in order to maintain the higher percentage of endurance work.)

Each year is based on three training periods: the base, transition, and racing seasons. The base period, in which aerobic strength is being improved, is the longest stage, running roughly from October through January. The transition phase introduces more VO_2 max and threshold workouts, and runs from February until May. Beginning in May, mileage is decreased and more economy intervals are introduced.

Although the weekly plans are presented on a Sunday through Saturday basis, not all walkers are able to maintain the daily schedule which is recommended. Again, you may make modifications, provided the schedule retains the same order. If you are forced to make random changes, try to follow the weekly and monthly pattern as closely as possible.

Metric and Mileage Measurements

Throughout the training schedules, suggested distances are given both in mileage and metric measurements with good reason: because most races are measured metrically, interval track workouts should also be computed in meters. However, most road workouts will be walked on courses measured in miles, which explains this inconsistency in the recommended training schedules. For those unfamiliar with metric/mileage equivalents, the following conversion chart includes the most important distances for race walkers in both miles and meters:

        400 meters = 436 yards
        800 meters = 873 yards
        1,609 meters = 1 mile
        3,000 meters = 1 mile, 1,513 yards
        5,000 meters = 3 miles, 175 yards
        10,000 meters = 6 miles, 350 yards

Planning Speeds and Workloads

Throughout the weekly schedules that follow, specific workouts will be suggested for raising the anaerobic threshold, increasing VO_2 max and improving economy. Each walker needs workouts that are aimed at improvement in these areas, but some walkers should stress certain types of workouts more than others. The training tables that follow are generally "all-purpose" programs, allowing for improvement in each area. Naturally, the more stressful VO_2 max and economy workouts are limited to the last few weeks before major races, due to the fact that performing these types of workouts for prolonged periods will lead to injury and breakdown.

Each walker needs to plan his or her own training sessions in these areas based on the formulas which are given below for each type of workout. It is important to follow the formulas closely, since stressful workouts that are performed too fast or too often will interfere with the process of progressive stress adaptation and increase the possibility of injury. When departing from the exact day-to day training schedule, as will invariably occur, be sure to leave at least 48 hours between anaerobic workouts. Athletes who are training at altitudes over 6,000 feet should decrease the pace of each workout to compensate for the effects of high altitude.

Threshold Training

Threshold interval training is designed to stress the body at levels in the upper end of the anaerobic threshold. By using these workouts to improve the body's ability to handle greater accumulations of lactacids, walkers will begin to raise their threshold and work in a range which is closer to their VO_2 max level.

Threshold training consists of long intervals, ranging from 3,000 meters to 5,000 meters in length, walked at a pace near the athlete's present 10,000 meter race pace. Rest periods between efforts should equal about 33% of the threshold interval time. Because threshold workouts are not as stressful as other types of training, they should be utilized throughout the training year.

The table below allows each walker to calculate his or her threshold workout including the pace and rest period. The recommended number of repetitions for each interval are given in the yearly training tables. The suggested "average pace" should be the average tempo of the total number of repeat intervals; the first efforts may be walked slower, and the final intervals faster, to achieve the desired average pace for the entire workout.

Threshold Interval Training —Table A

Current 10,000m Race Pace	Average Pace for 3,000m Repeats	Rest Period Between Efforts	Average Pace for 5,000m Repeats	Rest Period Between Repeats
42:30	13:30	4:00	22:30	7:00
45:00	14:15	4:15	23:45	7:30
47:30	15:00	4:30	25:00	7:45
50:00	15:45	4:45	26:15	8:00
52:30	16:30	5:00	27:30	8:15
55:00	17:15	5:15	28:45	8:30

VO_2 Max Training

Walkers who possess basically good style, but have trouble generating speed over short distances need to emphasize VO_2 max training. These workouts can be maintained throughout the training year, but prove most important during the transition and racing phases. This type of training should make up no more than 10 percent of the total weekly mileage, and only one VO_2 max session per week should be attempted.

VO_2 max intervals should be walked at a pace near the present VO_2 max, based on the current "all-out" 5,000 meter race pace. Each interval effort should measure between four and seven minutes in length, with shorter rest periods between. The sample workouts given in Table B will help you calculate your own VO_2 max training sessions.

VO$_2$ Max Interval Training —Table B

Current 5,000m Race Pace	Current Weekly Training Mileage	Average Pace for 1,000m Repeats	Number of 1,000m Repeats	Rest Period for 1,000m Repeats
20:00	80	3:55	11-13	3:30
21:00	70	4:10	9-11	3:45
22:00	60	4:20	10	4:00
23:00	60	4:30	10	4:10
24:00	50	4:40	7-9	4:25
25:00	40	4:50	6-7	4:35

Current 5,000m Race Pace	Current Weekly Training Mileage	Average Pace for 1 Mile Repeats	Number of 1 Mile Repeats	Rest Period for 1 Mile Repeats
20:00	80	6:20	8	5:00
21:00	70	6:40	7	5:20
22:00	60	7:00	6	5:30
23:00	60	7:20	6	5:45
24:00	50	7:40	5	6:00
25:00	40	8:00	4	6:15

Economy Workouts

Economy training imposes maximum adaptation and forces a walker's body beyond the point at which it now operates efficiently. When monitored by a laboratory stress test, certain walkers will show a greater accumulation of lactic acids than other athletes who are walking at the same pace, indicating a need to incorporate economy workouts into their schedule.

Because economy workouts are stressful, they should be limited to the late transition and racing periods of the training cycle and must only constitute about 6 percent of the total weekly mileage. Economy workouts consist of shorter intervals of less than four minutes in duration, with longer rest periods in between. The pace should be based on a walker's current 3,000 meter race time. Sample economy workouts in Table C will help you calculate your own economy interval training sessions.

Economy Interval Training—Table C

Current 3,000m Race Pace	Current Weekly Training Mileage	Average Pace for 400m Repeats	Number of 400m Repeats	Rest Periods for 400m Repeats
11:00	80	1:25-1:30	18-20	2:00
12:00	70	1:30-1:35	16-18	2:10
13:00	60	1:35-1:40	14-16	2:15
14:00	50	1:40-1:45	12	2:20
15:00	50	1:45-1:50	12	2:30
16:00	40	1:50-1:55	8-10	2:35

Current 3,000m Race Pace	Current Weekly Training Mileage	Average Pace for 800m Repeats	Number of 800m Repeats	Rest Periods for 800m Repeats
11:00	80	3:00-3:05	9-10	3:30
12:00	70	3:10-3:15	8-9	3:45
13:00	60	3:20-3:25	7-8	4:00
14:00	50	3:30-3:35	6	4:15
15:00	50	3:40-3:50	6	4:30
16:00	40	3:50-4:00	4-5	4:30

Other Workouts: Types and Tempos

In addition to workouts using the above formulas for precise distance and pace, many workouts will be described using terms such as "easy," "medium," and "hard." The tempos for these workouts are purposely left up to the individual walker, pace will depend on conditions and recovery from the previous day's workout. Walkers who are performing workouts designated as "easy" should work only in the aerobic range throughout the training session and watch for signs indicating that they are moving into the anaerobic state, such as heavy breathing and excessive perspiration. Walkers are meant to perform "medium" pace workouts in the upper ranges of the anaerobic threshold. Finally, "hard" workouts definitely suggest that a walker should be working in the anaerobic state.

Least precise of all are *fartlek* workouts. Fartlek, a Swedish word meaning "speed play," can be a threshold, VO₂ max, or economy-type workout, depending on the speed and rest periods. Fartlek workouts consist of harder efforts followed by easier walking to recover. A typical short fartlek workout might be as loosely organized as walking "fast" between every other telephone pole. This type of training is intended to provide good anaerobic workouts without requiring that a walker be too concerned with pace and distance ... "speed play," indeed.

Although hill work has not yet been mentioned, these workouts can play an important role in a training program. If a walker is living in an area of hilly terrain, he or she should use the hills whenever possible, especially during the base and transition phases of the yearly program. Whenever the day's plan calls for a workout that may be performed on the road, incorporate hill training if possible. Hill work builds the springing muscles of the body in addition to placing extra stress on the cardiovascular system. Easy, medium, hard or fartlek workouts all may be performed on hills.

As a season progresses, or certainly at the end of an entire season, the walker and coach should make an honest evaluation of progress and where the greatest potential for improvement lies. Are more VO₂ max or economy interval sessions needed? Were the long workouts too long, or should more mileage be added? These and many other questions must be decided in order to modify the following training schedules in an intelligent manner.

Supplemental training, such as stretching and mobility exercises, are an important part of any training program. Based on available training time, each walker should schedule periods for stretching exercises during workouts. Three flexibility and stretching sessions, each up to 30 minutes in length, should be included each week. Walkers with specific technique and/or strength improvement needs may need to work up to 30 minutes each day to overcome such deficiencies.

Training for Youth Walkers

A balance of sports— soccer in the fall, swimming in winter, race walking in the spring— is preferable for athletes who are under high school age. This balance will prove far more effective in fostering a healthy attitude towards sports and fitness than forcing a 12-months-of-the-year regimen of race walking on a young athlete.

Many young athletes (high school age and under), deciding to turn their attention to race walking in the spring, will find their club or school coaches resistant to the idea of this sport. This reluctance is usually due to the coach's lack of technical understanding of the sport and the fact that he or she does not have the knowledge to train athletes for race walking. Athletes may be required to plan their own training schedules, using the following program as a guide, or their coaches can put them on the same basic plan as the team's long distance runners. Because younger athletes rarely compete at distances more than 3,000 meters, most good distance running schedules will adequately prepare a walker who is training for the short distances in youth race walking, provided technique training is not neglected.

It is very important to expose young walkers to competent judging as early in their career as possible. Far too many young race walkers with good athletic futures have quit the sport as a result of their disappointment in being disqualified in a championship race. In the majority of these cases, the athletes have never been judged properly until they arrived at the championship race. As a consequence, their coaches and parents often conclude that race walking is a waste of time, and coach and athlete alike are lost to the sport.

At about age 16, a young walker may wish to become more single-minded in the pursuit of race walking excellence. Yet, even at this age, diversity should be encouraged; an ideal schedule for a young athlete might include cross-country running in the fall, wrestling or swimming in the winter and race walking beginning in early March. (Basketball is best avoided since sprained ankles can wipe out an entire track season.) This agenda allows the athlete time to prepare for distances approaching and including 10,000 meters. The following monthly schedule is designed for athletes who are training for such distances.

One-Year Training Plan for Youth Walkers

August-November:

Participate in cross-country training with a school or club track team.

December-February:

Take part in winter sports. If these programs are not available, walkers can begin mild race walking workouts twice per week and continue the running program. If an athlete is involved in other winter sports activities, one long walk per week is beneficial. The distance should not exceed 8 miles, with a pace no faster than 9:00 per mile.

March:

Assuming that the walker has achieved good basic condition as a result of the winter's routine, reinforcing legal race walking technique is the high priority of this month. As they prepare for distance events ranging up to 10,000 meters, walkers should follow the weekly schedule below.

Sunday	90:00 at easy pace.
Monday	Off.
Tuesday	1 hour at medium pace.
Wednesday	15:00 warm-up, followed by a 30:00 fartlek workout, using long efforts.
Thursday	1 hour at medium pace.
Friday	Off.
Saturday	Race; or 3,000m-5 mile time trial. Time trials should be performed at target race pace.

Mileage for a typical March training week=30 miles.

April:

One or two age-group meets may be entered during this month, but the basic training plan should not be altered to accommodate these races.

Sunday	90:00, increasing the pace throughout the month.
Monday	30:00 at easy pace.
Tuesday	15:00 warm-up, followed by 30:00 fartlek workout, using long efforts.
Wednesday	1 hour at easy pace.
Thursday	Mixed VO_2 and economy intervals; choose from: 6 X 800m, 4 X 1,000m, or 3 X 1 mile, all at faster than race pace. (An ideal interval workout for a youth walker might be arranged as follows: 1 mile warm-up; followed by 6 X 110m to prepare the body and mind for fast

walking; 3 X 1 mile at 8:00 per mile pace, with 8:00 strolls to rest between the miles; flexibility exercises and a 10:00 slow stroll to warm-down.)

Friday Off.

Saturday Race or 3,000m-5 mile time trial.

Mileage for a typical April training week=35 miles.

May:

The walker should increase intensity of workouts and target efforts toward one important competition during the month.

Sunday 10 miles; pace should vary depending on the intensity of Saturday's workout-faster if Saturday's workout was easy, slower if the previous session was harder and anaerobic.

Monday 30:00 at easy pace.

Tuesday Threshold intervals; choose from: 2 X 2,000m or 2 X 2 miles. (Refer to Table A on page 59 to determine pace and rest periods.)

Wednesday 1 hour at easy pace.

Thursday VO$_2$ max intervals, using 1,000m efforts. (Refer to Table B on page 60 to determine pace, number of repetitions and rest periods.)

Friday Off.

Saturday Race or 3,000m-5 mile time trial.

Mileage for a typical May training week=35 miles.

June-July:

Peak of racing season. Walkers may be compete as often as every weekend.

Sunday 90:00 at hard pace. If distance of the previous day's race exceeded 3,000m, cut workout time to 1 hour.

Monday 30:00 at easy pace, ending with 4 X 110m sprints.

Tuesday Economy intervals; choose from: 4-6 X 800m, 8-10 X 440m, 12-15 X 220m, or *stepladder* (200m-400-800-800-400-200).

Wednesday 30:00 at easy pace.

> *Thursday* Economy intervals; choose a different
> set from Tuesday's workout than
> performed previously. If racing a 3,000m
> or greater distance on Saturday, cut the
> number of intervals to make the
> workout less stressful.
> *Friday* Off, unless racing 10,000m on Saturday;
> in this event, do some light strolling.
> *Saturday* Race; or 5,000m time trial.
> *Mileage for a typical June-July training*
> *week=25 to 30 miles.*

Younger athletes who have already achieved success in
10,000m racing, may wish to follow a more challenging
program, such as the schedules for 10,000m training given
in the next section.

Training for 10,000 Meters

The primary racing distance for women, junior men
and the N.A.I.A. championships is 10,000 meters. While
these athletes may wish to race seriously in longer distance
events, the following training program is designed for
those walkers who are specifically preparing for the 10,000
meter distance and the most important racing season for
this event— late May through mid-July. This season
includes the N.A.I.A. Championship, Women's Nationals,
Junior Championships and perhaps a series of Junior dual
meets. In addition, top-level women walkers may qualify
for the Eschborn Cup, the international 10,000 meter
competition held as part of the I.A.A.F. World Cup team
competitions, which traditionally take place in late
September.

Because the demands of training for 10,000 meter
racing are not as complex as for 20 and 50 kilometer
distances, less attention has been devoted to training plans
spanning several seasons. This is not to degrade the 10,000
meter athletes or the severity of their training schedules; it
is simply a fact of adaptation that training for 20 and 50
kilometers requires more work in all areas— technique,
endurance, speed, strength and flexibility.

Ten thousand meter walkers can use the following
schedule for several seasons over a one-year period,
improving the quality of the workouts from season to
season.

One-Year Plan for 10,000 Meter Training

Overview: Weekly Mileage Totals Per Month:

October	45
November	45
December	60
January	60
February	60
March	60
April	50
May	45
June	40
August	Varies, depending upon racing goals.
September	45

September-November:
Off-season, except for those walkers participating in major competitions, such as the Eschborn Cup. Juniors and N.A.I.A. walkers may wish to run with their cross-country teams even if they are not participating on the varsity level. Although maintaining a walking program is more effective, such off-season running is acceptable for walkers aiming at 10,000m. High-mileage walking base training is not a priority. Those walking during this period should train by the following weekly schedule:

Sunday	2 hours, covering about 12 miles.
Monday	30:00 at easy pace.
Tuesday	1 hour at medium pace.
Wednesday	15:00 warm-up, followed by a fartlek workout, using long efforts: 3 X 8:00-12:00, totaling at least 1 hour of walking, including the rest periods between hard efforts.
Thursday	1 hour at easy pace.
Friday	Off.
Saturday	Threshold intervals: 2 X 5,000m. (Refer to Table A on page 59 to determine pace and rest periods.)

December-February
Do not compete in more than one race per month, or in distances exceeding 20km. If shifting from a cross-country running schedule, follow the September-

November program for the first month of walking training.

Sunday	2 hours, covering 12 to 13 miles.
Monday	1 hour; pace should depend on the intensity of Sunday's workout.
Tuesday	Fartlek workout, using long efforts similar to September-November fartlek schedule.
Wednesday	90:00; first 60:00 at easy pace, and final 30:00 at hard pace.
Thursday	1 hour at medium pace.
Friday	Off.
Saturday	Threshold intervals; choose from 2 X 5,000m or 4 X 2,500m. (Refer to Table A on page 59 to determine pace and rest periods.)

March-April:

You may enter three 5,000-10,000m races and one longer race during this two-month period, but special racing preparation and training time outside the regular schedule should be held to a minimum.

Sunday	2 hours, covering 12 to 13 miles.
Monday	30:00 warm-up, followed by VO_2 max intervals of 1 mile. (Refer to Table B on page 60 to determine pace, number of repetitions and rest periods.)
Tuesday	90:00 at easy pace.
Wednesday	Threshold intervals: 3 X 5,000m. (Refer to Table A on page 59 to determine pace and rest periods.)
Thursday	1 hour at easy pace.
Friday	Off or easy strolling.
Saturday	Race; or a 4-5 mile time trial on track at race pace.

May:

The most important races for many collegiate walkers— District and National Championships— take place during May, while the most critical races for women and junior walkers are usually held in June. Workouts for this month will vary, according to your particular racing schedule.

Sunday	90:00, covering 10 1/2 -11 miles.
Monday	4 mile time trial at race pace or faster.

Tuesday   90:00 at easy pace.

Wednesday   May racers use economy intervals; choose from: 12 X 400m, 10 X 600m or 8 X 800m. June racers use VO_2 max intervals; choose from 5 X 1,000m or 4 X 1 mile. (Refer to Tables B and C on pages 60 and 61 to determine paces and rest periods.

Thursday   1 hour at medium pace.

Friday   Off.

Saturday   Race; or 4-7 miles at medium pace.

June-July:

Prime racing season. Because 10,000m racers require less recovery time than longer distance athletes, it is possible to race quite often with success during this period.

Sunday   90:00 at medium pace.

Monday   Off or easy strolling.

Tuesday VO_2 max intervals; choose a set from May's schedule with fewer intervals than performed previously and work at faster pace per Table B.

Wednesday   1 hour at medium pace.

Thursday   Short economy intervals; choose a set from May's schedule with fewer intervals than performed previously and work at faster pace per Table C.

Friday   Off.

Saturday   Race; or 5,000m-5 mile time trial.

August-September

If competing in the Eschborn Cup in the fall, follow April's schedule during August, shifting to the June-July schedule for September. If no major races are scheduled for these months, use the time to compete often in local races, training under the June-July schedule.

Training for 20 and 50 Kilometers

Beginning a training program aimed at the Olympic distances— 20 and 50 kilometers— is a step which all male walkers must take if they are truly serious about the sport.

1. 2.

5. 6.

9. 10.

In the sequence photographs shown above, young walkers display a variety of arm and body carriages during the 1984 U.S. Junior Championship 10 kilometer race. Note the predominance of rigid upper bodies and the long ranges of arm motions. (Photo by Tom Carroll.)

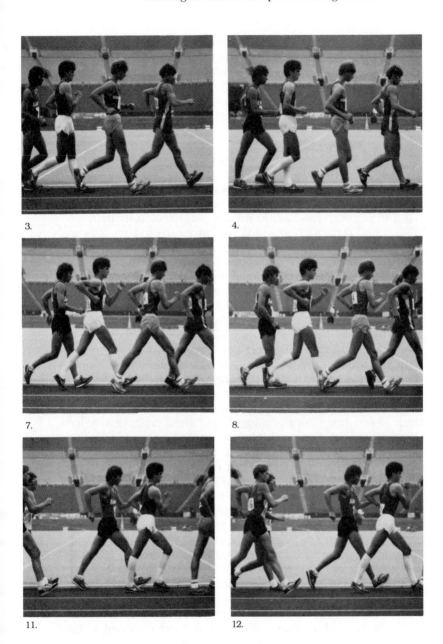

3.

4.

7.

8.

11.

12.

For many walkers, who have been competing at 10,000 meters and shorter distances during their entire race walking career, 20 kilometers may seem like a formidable distance, and 50 kilometers might be a distance they would not even like to consider. But, as athletes intensify training and gain strength to handle such distances, it is soon realized that 20 kilometers really is a "sprint distance" and 50 kilometers can be mastered.

Many walkers do not realize that moving from the 10 kilometer to the 20 kilometer distance, or from the "20" to the "50," does not require an enormous increase in training time. Even continuing the same training program that is used to prepare for 10,000 meters will eventually provide walkers with enough stamina and strength to race 20s with fair success. Likewise, a few seasons of consistent 20 kilometer training eventually will allow athletes to walk a fairly respectable 50 kilometer time.

There are drawbacks, however, to racing longer distance events without devoting specialized training time to preparation. While many walkers will be able to achieve a good time in their first longer distance race, their physical condition will deteriorate from this effort to such a degree that it may be months before they recover enough to repeat such a time and performance. This is a common occurrence in trial races. A walker may win a spot on a team which competes in a longer racing distance event than his or her training allows, and then walk poorly in the major meet. Such athletes do not fail because they "choke" or slacken their effort in the major race, as spectators frequently think, but rather because they have not recovered from the all-out effort that was required to qualify for the team in the first place.

Training should be as "distance-specific" as possible to maximize chances to make the team initially, as well as ensure good performance in the finals. By distance-specific, we mean that athletes should plan their training schedules according to the depletion work, ability to handle lactacid energy, and other strengths which a particular racing distance will require.

Such distance-specific, three-year training plans for both the 20 and 50 kilometer distances are outlined in the next several pages. These programs are aimed at helping a walker begin and continue intelligent and goal-oriented training practices for a three-year period, culminating in world-class performance at the Olympic games.

A few words of explanation:

* The training programs are designed on the basis that a 20 kilometer walker begins the three-year training cycle with the conditioning to finish the distance in approximately 1:35.00. Fifty kilometer walkers should be able to finish their distance within about 4:30.00 before undertaking the program. Walkers who have yet to achieve this conditioning should scale the workouts back accordingly.

* Of course, not every walker using these tables will have a three-year time period until the next Olympic games. The tables can be modified to fit an athletes' actual amount of training time before a major competitive event. Walkers should choose the yearly training schedule that best matches their 20 or 50 kilometer time and conditioning. For example: An athlete begins training approximately one year before the target event. In his present level of conditioning, the athlete can finish a 20 kilometer race in 1:28.00. This walker should choose to follow the tables for Year Two of 20 kilometer training, since these workouts best reflect his current capabilities. Attempting to follow the tables for Year Three may result in injury simply because the body does not possess the strength to handle the recommended workload.

* As we mentioned in the introduction, the tempos of the fast-paced workouts will either be geared to VO_2 max or economy pace. It is not necessary to see significant improvements in similar workouts from one week to the next. Rather, times should improve on a month-to-month basis as the season progresses. Refer to the explanations of these workouts above in "Planning Speeds and Workloads" to determine pace.

* Do not be afraid to take extra time off from the schedule to recover and rest for a major upcoming race. No depletion work should be performed closer than 10 days before a race exceeding 20 kilometers, and no lactacid work should be scheduled closer than four days. During the last few days before a major competition, a few fast 100 meter sprints and strolling sessions are sufficient to keep the snap in your legs. After a major competition over such

distances, wait at least one to two weeks before resuming regular anaerobic and long distance workouts.

- When recovering from major races, or very hard, anaerobic workouts, check your morning pulse before resuming hard training. Until the morning pulse returns to its usual rate, no depletion or anaerobic workouts should be attempted, regardless of the schedule.

- Although they are not specified in the schedules, planned rest periods are vital to maintaining a healthy training program. Walkers should set aside an "easy week" every four to six weeks. Reduce the intensity of workouts to about half of the intensity of the previous week's sessions, and use this period to refresh yourself mentally and physically. Your body will use the recovery time to adapt to the stress of past training.

- More difficult workouts should be scheduled for the afternoon or evening, unless you know that you are "loose" in the morning and/or can warm up easily at this time. Morning workouts may be added to the schedules to increase mileage, but they should not be so difficult that they interfere with the evening session. If a walker is injury-prone during speed workouts, or has trouble warming up, morning workouts are important on the day of a speed-training session. Thirty minutes to one hour of strolling at a comfortable pace should suffice to warm up muscles and joints for an evening of speed work.

- The training programs are based on what has proven to be typical seasons, conforming to the schedule of major trials and races in May and June, and major world championships in late summer and early fall. Variations from this racing schedule may occur, and individual walkers and their coaches must adapt the workouts accordingly.

Three-Year Plan for 20 Kilometer Training

Overview: Weekly Mileage Totals Per Month:

	Year One	Year Two	Year Three
November	50	55	70
December	60	65	80
January	70	80	80
February	70	85	85
March	60	75	80
April	55	70	80
May	55	70	75
June	50	60	60
July	50	65	65
August	50	65	65
September	50	65	60
October	rest	rest	
20 Kilometer Time Goal:	1:28.00	1:25.00	1:22.00

Weekly Training Schedule for Each Month of the First Year
20 Kilometer Time Goal: 1:28.00

November:

Sunday	2 hours at easy pace.
Monday	1 hour at medium pace.
Tuesday	1 hour at easy pace.
Wednesday	90:00, increasing speed every 30:00.
Thursday	1 hour fartlek workout, using long efforts.
Friday	Off.
Saturday	2 X 5000m; first interval at easy pace, followed by a 5:00 rest period and 1 interval at hard pace.

Total mileage: 50

December:

Sunday	3 hours at easy pace.
Monday	7 miles at medium pace.
Tuesday	90:00 at medium pace.
Wednesday	1 hour at easy pace.
Thursday	90:00, increasing speed every 30:00.
Friday	Off.

     Saturday 2 X 5000m at easy/hard paces, with a
             5:00 rest period.

Total mileage: 60

January:

     Sunday 20 miles; 9:00 per mile pace.
     Monday 7 miles at medium pace.
     Tuesday 90:00 at easy pace.
  Wednesday 10 miles; 8:15 per mile pace.
    Thursday 90:00; long fartlek workout for the last
             45:00 (3 X 10:00 with 5:00 rest periods).
      Friday Off.
    Saturday Threshold intervals: 2 X 5,000m. (Refer
             to Table A on page 59 to determine pace
             and rest periods.)

Total mileage: 70

February:

     Sunday 20 miles; 8:30 per mile pace.
     Monday 7 miles at medium pace.
     Tuesday 90:00 at easy pace.
  Wednesday 2 hours, increasing speed every 30:00.
    Thursday Threshold intervals; choose from
             6 X 2,000m, 5 X 2,500m or 4 X 3,000m.
             (Refer to Table A on page 59 to determine
             pace and rest period.)
      Friday Off.
    Saturday 2 X 7,500m at medium/hard paces, with
             10:00 rest period.

Total mileage: 70

March:

     Sunday 20 miles; 8:30 per mile pace.
     Monday 1 hour at easy pace.
     Tuesday 10 miles; 8:00 per mile pace.
  Wednesday 1 hour at easy pace.
    Thursday Threshold intervals; choose from the
             same sets of intervals as outlined for
             February, but work at faster pace per
             Table A.
      Friday Off.
    Saturday 2 X 5,000m at slow/medium paces, with
             5:00 rest period.

Total mileage: 60

April:

     Sunday   20 miles; 8:15-8:30 per mile pace.
     Monday   1 hour at medium pace.
     Tuesday   Threshold intervals; choose from the same sets of intervals as outlined for February.
     Wednesday   10 miles; 8:30 per mile pace.
     Thursday VO_2 intervals; choose from 6 X 1,000m or 3 X 2,000m. (Refer to training Table B on page 60 to determine pace and rest periods.)
     Friday   Off.
     Saturday   Threshold intervals: 2 X 5,000m at pace per Table A.
     Total mileage: 55

May:

     Sunday   20 miles; 8:15-8:30 per mile pace.
     Monday   1 hour at medium pace.
     Tuesday VO_2 max intervals; choose from same intervals as outlined for April's Thursday workout, but walk at faster pace per Table B.
     Wednesday   1 hour at easy pace.
     Thursday   Economy intervals; choose from 6-8 X 800m, 10-12 X 400m, or stepladder (200, 400, 800, 800, 400, 200; repeat). Refer to Table C on page 61 to determine pace and rest periods.
     Friday   Off.
     Saturday   Threshold intervals, with 6:00 rest periods.
     Total mileage: 55

June:

     Sunday   15 miles; 7:50-8:00 per mile pace.
     Monday   1 hour at medium pace.
     Tuesday   Short economy intervals; choose from same sets of intervals as outlined for May's Thursday workout, but walk at faster pace.
     Wednesday   90:00 at easy pace.
     Thursday   Threshold intervals: 3 X 3,000m. (Refer

to Table A on page 59 to determine pace
and rest periods.)
Friday   Off or easy strolling.
Saturday   1 hour at easy pace, with repetition of
fast 200m or 300ms during the final
15:00.
Total mileage: 55

July-September:

Repeat June's schedule, breaking for races. As usual,
check the pulse rate after each race to determine when
to resume regular training.

Because economy and VO_2 max intervals are
stressful, these workouts should not be done for an
extended period the same week, as is called for in
June's schedule. During the July, August and
September period, it is best to alternate these types of
interval workouts from one week to the next. For
instance, perform an economy workout during the
first week of July, a VO_2 max workout the second week,
an economy workout the third and so on.

Weekly Training Schedule for Each Month of the Second Year
20 Kilometer Time Goal: 1:25.00

November:

Sunday   2 ½ hours at easy pace; approximately
17 miles.
Monday   1 hour at easy pace.
Tuesday   2 hours at medium pace.
Wednesday   1 hour at medium pace.
Thursday   15:00 warm-up, followed by 1 hour
fartlek workout, using long efforts.
Friday   Off.
Saturday   Threshold intervals: 2 X 5,000m. (Refer
to Table A on page 59 to determine pace
and rest periods.)
Total mileage: 55

December:

Sunday   3 hours at easy pace.
Monday   1 hour at medium pace.
Tuesday   90:00 on a hilly course at medium pace.

Wednesday 1 hour fartlek workout, using long
efforts.
Thursday 2 hours, increasing speed every 30:00.
Friday Off.
Saturday Threshold intervals: 3 X 5,000m. (Refer
to Table A on page 59 to determine pace
and rest periods.)
Total mileage: 65

January:

Sunday 35km; 9:00 per mile pace.
Monday 7 miles; sub-8:30 per mile pace.
Tuesday 90:00 on a hilly course at easy pace.
Wednesday 20km; 8:15-8:30 per mile pace.
Thursday 90:00; 1st hour at easy pace; fartlek
workout for the final 30:00, using long
efforts.
Friday 1 hour at easy pace.
Saturday Threshold intervals: 3 X 5,000m. (Refer
to Table A on page 59 to determine pace
and rest periods.
Total Mileage: 80

February:

Sunday 35km; 8:30 per mile pace.
Monday 7 miles; 8:00 per mile pace.
Tuesday 90:00 on a hilly course at easy pace.
Wednesday 2 hours, increasing speed every 30:00.
Thursday Threshold intervals; choose from
6 X 2,000m, 5 X 2,500m or 4 X 3,000m
efforts at pace per Table A
Friday 90:00 at easy pace.
Saturday Threshold intervals: 3 X 5,000m.
Total mileage: 85

March:

Sunday 20 miles; 8:30-8:45 per mile pace (35 km;
8:30 per mile pace once per month)
Monday 1 hour at easy pace.
Tuesday 7 miles; 7:45 per mile pace.
Wednesday 90:00 stroll; first hour at easy pace;
fartlek workout for the final 30:00, using
long efforts.
Thursday Threshold intervals; choose from same

	sets of intervals as outlined for February's Thursday workout.
Friday	1 hour at easy pace.
Saturday	3 X 5,000m at easy/medium/hard paces, walking 1 interval every 30:00.

Total mileage: 75

April:

Sunday	20 miles; 8:15-8:30 per mile pace.
Monday	1 hour at easy pace.
Tuesday	1 hour at medium pace.
Wednesday	90 minute stroll; 1st hour at easy pace, increasing speed every 30:00.
Thursday	VO$_2$ max intervals, using 1 mile efforts. (Refer to Table B on page 60 to determine pace, number of repetitions and rest periods.)
Friday	1 hour at easy pace.
Saturday	3 X 5,000m at easy/medium/hard paces, walking 1 interval every 30:00.

Total mileage: 70

May:

Sunday	20 miles; 8:00-8:30 per mile pace.
Monday	1 hour at easy pace.
Tuesday	VO$_2$ max intervals, using 1,000m efforts.
Wednesday	90:00, increasing speed for the final 30:00.
Thursday	Threshold intervals: 5 X 3000m. (Refer to the Table A on page 59 to determine pace and rest periods.)
Friday	1 hour at easy pace.
Saturday	1 hour at medium pace.

Total mileage: 70

June:

Nationals/Trials.

Sunday	15 miles; 8:00 per mile pace.
Monday	1 hour at easy pace.
Tuesday	Economy intervals, using 400m and 800m efforts. (Refer to Table C on page 61 to determine pace, number of repetitions and rest periods.)
Wednesday	90:00, increasing speed for the final

30:00. Finish off with repetitions of a
few fast 200m and 300m.

Thursday   VO₂ max intervals, using 1,000m efforts.
Friday   Off.
Saturday   1 hour at medium pace.
Total mileage: 60

July:

Sunday   20 miles; 8:00-8:30 per mile pace.
Monday   1 hour at easy pace.
Tuesday   Economy intervals, using 400 and 800m
efforts. (Use economy workouts no more
than 8 consecutive weeks. For a break,
substitute 1 hour at medium pace on this
day.)
Wednesday   90:00 at easy pace.
Thursday   Off or easy strolling.
Friday   VO₂ max intervals, using 1,000m efforts.
Saturday   1 hour at medium pace.
Total mileage: 65

August & September:

Repeat July's schedule, aiming for the Lugano Cup
in late September. Walkers will probably race 2-3 times
per month in this period, but should not participate in
races that exceed 30km because of the needed recovery
time.

Weekly Training Schedule for Each Month
of the Third (Olympic) Year
20 Kilometer Time Goal: 1:22.00

November:

Sunday   3 hours at easy pace.
Monday   7 miles; 8:30 per mile pace.
Tuesday   1 hour at easy pace.
Wednesday   2 hours at medium pace.
Thursday   90:00; fartlek workout for the final
30:00, using long efforts.
Friday   Off.
Saturday   2 X 7,500m at easy/medium paces, with
10:00 rest period.
Total mileage: 70

December:

Sunday	35km; 8:30-8:45 per mile pace.
Monday	7 miles; 8:15 per mile pace.
Tuesday	1 hour at easy pace.
Wednesday	2 hours, increasing speed for the second hour.
Thursday	90:00; fartlek workout for the final 45:00, using long efforts.
Friday	1 hour at easy pace.
Saturday	2 X 7,500m at medium/hard paces, with 10:00 rest period.

Total mileage: 80

January:

Sunday	35km; 8:30 per mile pace.
Monday	1 hour at medium pace.
Tuesday	90:00 on hilly course at easy pace.
Wednesday	20km; 8:15 per mile pace.
Thursday	90:00; fartlek workout for the final hour, using a combination of short and long efforts.
Friday	Off or easy strolling.
Saturday	Threshold intervals: 3 X 5,000m. (Refer to Table A on page 59 to determine pace and rest periods.)

Total mileage: 80

February:

Sunday	35km; 8:15-8:30 per mile pace.
Monday	1 hour at easy pace.
Tuesday	Threshold intervals: 4 X 3,000m. (Refer to Table A on page 59 to determine pace and rest periods.)
Wednesday	10 miles; 8:00-8:30 per mile pace.
Thursday	90:00 on hilly course at easy pace.
Friday	1 hour at easy pace.
Saturday	Threshold intervals: 2 X 5,000m at pace per Table A.

Total mileage: 85

March:

Sunday	20 miles; 8:15 per mile pace.
Monday	1 hour at easy pace.
Tuesday	Threshold intervals: 5 X 3,000m. (Refer

to Table A on page 59 to determine pace
and rest periods.)
Wednesday 10 miles; 8:00-8:30 per mile pace.
Thursday 90:00 at medium pace on hilly course.
Friday 1 hour at easy pace.
Saturday Threshold intervals: 3 X 5,000m at pace
per Table A.
Total mileage: 80

April:
Sunday 20 miles; 8:15 per mile pace.
Monday 1 hour at easy pace.
Tuesday 90:00; fartlek workout for the final
30:00, using short efforts.
Wednesday 10 miles; 8:30 per mile pace.
Thursday VO$_2$ max intervals, using 1 mile efforts.
(Refer to Table B on page 60 to determine
pace, number of repetitions and rest
periods.)
Friday 1 hour at easy pace.
Saturday Threshold intervals: 3 X 5,000m at pace
per Table A.
Total mileage: 80

May:
Sunday 20 miles; 8:00-8:15 per mile pace.
Monday 1 hour at easy pace.
Tuesday Economy intervals, using 800m efforts.
(Refer to Table C on page 61 to determine
pace, number of repetitions and rest
periods.)
Wednesday 1 hour at easy pace.
Thursday VO$_2$ max intervals, using 1,000m efforts
at pace per Table B
Friday 90:00 at easy pace.
Saturday 2 X 5000m at easy/hard paces, with 5:00
rest period.
Total mileage: 75

June:
Olympic trials. Reduce distance and increase tempo
during the days approaching the race.
Sunday 15 miles; 7:45-8:00 per mile pace.
Monday 1 hour at easy pace.
Tuesday Economy intervals, using 400 and 800m

efforts. (Refer to Table C on page 61 to
determine pace, number of repetitions
and rest periods.)

Wednesday 90:00 at medium pace.
Thursday 1 hour at easy pace.
Friday VO₂ max intervals, using 1,000m efforts
at pace per Table B.
Saturday 1 hour at medium pace.
Total mileage: 60

July

Sunday 20 miles; 8:30 per mile pace.
Monday 1 hour at easy pace.
Tuesday Economy intervals, using 400m and
800m efforts. Refer to Table C on page 61
to determine pace, number of repetitions
and rest periods. (Use economy intervals
no more than 8 consecutive weeks. For a
break, substitute 1 hour at medium pace.)
Wednesday 10 miles; 8:30-9:00 per mile pace.
Thursday VO₂ max intervals, using 1,000m efforts
at pace per Table B.
Friday Off or easy strolling.
Saturday 1 hour at medium pace.
Total mileage: 65

August:
Probable Olympic games month. Repeat July's
schedule, increasing tempo of timed workouts, but
cutting down distances and number of interval
repetitions as race date draws closer. Continue to refer
to formulas for workouts specified as threshold,
economy or VO₂ max.

Training for 50 Kilometers

An athlete who is training for the 50 kilometer (31
miles) distance must be prepared to make sacrifices in
lifestyle. Leading a "normal life" while training seriously
for this event is almost impossible, due to the mental and
physical stresses of the event.

Considering the rewards which are commonly given to
winning athletes involved in more popular sports and the
usual lack of such rewards in race walking, both
nationally and internationally, one might begin to
question why anyone would wish to attack this event

seriously. The practical answer is that there is great opportunity for success, since few athletes will make the commitment needed for success in 50 kilometer competition.

On a more idealistic level, the "50" poses enormous challenges, physically and mentally, and the respect one can gain from informed track fans, as well as from the walking community, is enormous. And yes, it is possible to enjoy training, even for this most demanding of events.

Athletes who have seriously trained for race walking for more than a couple of years should make an attempt at walking a 50 to find what talent they may have for competing in the distance. A period of one year— from the end of one competitive season (August) through the trials for next year's international meets— should be the minimum commitment. Even if an athlete does not achieve the desired results, this base of training will prove beneficial in mastering the 20 kilometer event.

The decision to attack the 50 kilometer distance usually is not made this carefully. Few athletes start their careers to become 50 kilometer specialists, but many eventually find that their talent lies in this event. There *are* certain attributes that are very important to mastering this distance.

- *Durability* in mind and body is the most valuable asset that a walker can possess. The mileage and accompanying time requirements place many demands on the body. Motivating oneself to train at all times of the year and under all conditions requires a great deal of self-discipline.
- *Efficient, fair technique* is even more important to master for the 50 kilometer walker than it is for sprint racing counterparts. Fatigue tends to maximize style problems, such as bent knees, and technique fails as the 50 drags on. The anguish of a disqualification call is made even more bitter after months of training for a major race. Inefficient style, even if legal, is more likely to result in slower times and injuries during a race of this distance, since more energy is used to maintain poor technique. Furthermore, judging in the 50 kilometer event has proven to be more severe than at the 20 kilometer distance, with style problems more likely to result in disqualification.

1.

2.

3.

4.

5.

6.

American walker Marco Evonuik demonstrates the aggressive, powerful technique which brought him to a dominant victory in the 1984 Olympic trials 50 kilometer event. Note the strong ankle flexion, forward lean and forward hip rotation. Excessive upper body tension and a high forward arm drive are the flaws that keep his technique from being picture-perfect. (Photos by Tom Carroll.)

Three-Year Plan for 50 Kilometer Training
Overview: Weekly Mileage Totals Per Month

	Year One	Year Two	Year Three
November	70	70	80
December	80	80	100
January	90	110	115
February	90	110	115
March	90	110	110
April	80	80	95
May	70	80	85
June	70	90	75
July	70	75	70
August	70	65	Olympic games
September	70	65	
October	Active Rest	Active Rest	
50 Kilometer Time Goal	4:15.00	4:05.00	3:50.00

Weekly Training Schedule for Each Month of the First Year
50 Kilometer Time Goal: 4:15.00

November:

Sunday	20 miles; 10:00 per mile pace.
Monday	5 miles at medium pace.
Tuesday	25km; 9:00 per mile pace.
Wednesday	1 hour at easy pace.
Thursday	25km; 8:45 per mile pace.
Friday	Off.
Saturday	6 miles; 8:30 per mile pace.

Total mileage: 70

December:

Sunday	20 miles at easy pace.
Monday	5 miles at medium pace.
Tuesday	25km; 9:00 per mile pace.
Wednesday	1 hour at easy pace.
Thursday	25km; 8:45 per mile pace.
Friday	Off.
Saturday	6 miles; 8:30 per mile pace.

Total mileage: 80

January:

     Sunday   35km; 9:00 per mile pace. One Sunday during the month, switch to 4 hours at easy pace.

     Monday 10 miles; 9:00 per mile pace.

     Tuesday 25km; 8:30-8:45 per mile pace.

 Wednesday 90:00; fartlek workout for the final 30:00, using long efforts.

    Thursday 25km; 8:30-8:45 per mile pace.

       Friday Off.

    Saturday 6 miles; 8:30 per mile pace.

 Total mileage: 90

February:

     Sunday   35km; 8:45-9:00 per mile pace. One Sunday during the month, switch to 4 hours at the same pace.

     Monday 10 miles; 8:30 per mile pace.

     Tuesday 25km; 9:00 per mile pace.

 Wednesday 1 hour at medium pace.

    Thursday 30km; 9:00 per mile pace.

       Friday Off.

    Saturday 6 miles; 8:15-8:30 per mile pace.

 Total mileage: 90

March:

    Repeat February's schedule, increasing the intensity of the workouts each week.

April:

     Sunday   35km, slightly increasing speed each week, but not exceeding 8:30 per mile pace.

     Monday 1 hour at easy pace.

     Tuesday 10 miles; 8:30-9:00 per mile pace.

 Wednesday Threshold intervals; choose from 5 X 3000m or 3 X 5000m. (Refer to Table A on page 59 to determine pace and rest periods.)

    Thursday 1 hour at medium pace.

       Friday 90:00 at easy pace.

    Saturday 10 miles; 8:30-9:00 per mile pace.

 Total mileage: 80

May:

     Sunday   20 miles; 8:30-9:00 per mile pace; One

Sunday during the month, switch to 25-30 miles at easy pace.

Monday 1 hour at medium pace.
Tuesday 20km; 8:45 per mile pace.
Wednesday 1 hour at easy pace.
Thursday VO₂ max intervals, using 1 mile efforts. (Refer to Table B on page 60 to determine pace, number of repetitions and rest periods.)
Friday 90:00 at easy pace.
Saturday 10 miles; 8:30-9:00 per mile pace.
Total mileage: 70

June:

Sunday 15 miles; 8:15-8:30 per mile pace. Alternate with 20 mile workouts throughout the month; 8:30-9:00 per mile pace.
Monday 1 hour at easy pace.
Tuesday 2 hours at medium pace.
Wednesday 10 miles; 8:30-9:00 per mile pace.
Thursday Economy intervals, using 800m efforts. (Refer to Table C on page 61 to determine pace, number of repetitions and rest periods.)
Friday 1 hour at easy pace.
Saturday 90:00 at medium pace.
Total mileage: 70

July, August & September:
Maintain a schedule similar to June's program. If the above schedule has been followed, it should be possible to race four 50km or six 20km races during this period (including June). Economy workouts should be used no more than 8 consecutive weeks. No special compensation in the regular training program is needed for races under 15 km in length.

Weekly Training Schedule for Each Month of the Second Year
50 Kilometer Time Goal: 4:05.00

November:
Sunday 20 miles; 10:00 per mile pace.

>   *Monday* 5 miles at medium pace.
>   *Tuesday* 25km; 9:00 per mile pace.
>   *Wednesday* 1 hour at easy pace.
>   *Thursday* 25km; 8:45 per mile pace.
>   *Friday* Off.
>   *Saturday* 6 miles; 8:15-8:30 per mile pace.
>   *Total mileage: 70*

December:

>   *Sunday* 20 miles; 9:00 per mile pace. One Sunday
>   during the month, switch to 25 miles at
>   easy pace.
>   *Monday* 1 hour at medium pace.
>   *Tuesday* 25km; 8:15 per mile pace.
>   *Wednesday* 1 hour at easy pace.
>   *Thursday* 3 hours; faster than Sunday's pace.
>   *Friday* Off.
>   *Saturday* 6 miles; 8:15-8:20 per mile pace.
>   *Total mileage: 80*

January:

>   *Sunday* 35km; 8:45-9:00 per mile pace. One
>   Sunday during the month, switch to 4-5
>   hours at easy pace.
>   *Monday* 10 miles; 9:00 per mile pace.
>   *Tuesday* 30km; begin at easy pace, increasing
>   speed every 5km.
>   *Wednesday* 90:00 at easy pace.
>   *Thursday* 1 hour at medium pace.
>   *Friday* 3 X 5,000m at slow/medium/hard paces,
>   with 10:00 rest periods.
>   *Saturday* 1 hour at medium pace.
>   *Total mileage: 110*

February & March:
    Follow January's schedule, increasing intensity of
workouts as weeks progress. One or two "rest weeks"
should be inserted to allow for physical and mental
recovery.

April:

>   *Sunday* 20 miles; 8:30 per mile pace; One Sunday
>   during the month, switch to 4 hours at
>   easy pace.
>   *Monday* 1 hour at medium pace.

Tuesday   20km, increasing speed every 5km; overall time of sub-1:40.00
Wednesday   Threshold intervals at 50km target race pace of 4:05.00; 4 X 5,000m with 6:00 rest periods.
Thursday   10 miles; 8:30-9:00 per mile pace.
Friday   1 hour at medium pace.
Saturday   7 miles; 7:30 per mile pace.
Total mileage: 80

May:

Prepare for Lugano Cup Trials this month and World Track and Field Championships in August.

Sunday   35 km; 8:30 per mile pace.
Monday   1 hour at easy pace.
Tuesday   90:00 at medium pace.
Wednesday   VO$_2$ max intervals, using 1 mile efforts. (Refer to Table B on page 60 to determine pace, number of repetitions and rest periods.)
Thursday   90:00; begin at easy pace and increase speed every 30:00.
Friday   1 hour at easy pace.
Saturday   1 hour at medium pace.
Total mileage: 75

June:

Sunday   35km; 8:30-8:45 per mile pace. One Sunday during the month, switch to 50km; overall time of 4:30.00.
Monday   1 hour at easy pace.
Tuesday   90:00 at easy pace, increasing speed for the final 30:00.
Wednesday   VO$_2$ max intervals, using 1,000m efforts. (Refer to Table B on page 60 to determine pace, number of repetitions and rest periods.)
Thursday   2 hours at medium pace.
Friday   90:00, increasing speed every 30:00.
Saturday   1 hour at medium pace.
Total mileage: 90

July:

Sunday   35km; 8:20-8:40 per mile pace. One

Sunday during the month, switch to 50km; overall time of sub-4:20.00.

Monday 1 hour at easy pace.

Tuesday Economy intervals, using 800m efforts. (Refer to Table C on page 61 to determine pace, number of repetitions and rest periods.)

Wednesday 2 hours at easy pace.

Thursday Threshold intervals; 3 X 5,000m at pace per Table A.

Friday 1 hour at easy pace.

Saturday 10 miles; 8:30 per mile pace.

Total mileage: 75

August:

World Track and Field Championships at the end of the month. Reduce the intensity of workouts in the weeks approaching the Championships.

Sunday 25 miles; 8:30 per mile pace, dropping 3 miles per week and increasing pace.

Monday 1 hour at medium pace.

Tuesday VO_2 max intervals. using 1,000m efforts. (Refer to Table B on page 60 to determine pace, number of repetitions and rest periods.)

Wednesday 1 hour at easy pace.

Thursday Economy intervals, using 400m and 800m efforts at pace per Table C.

Friday 90:00 at easy pace.

Saturday 1 hour at medium pace.

Total mileage: 65

September:

Prepare for the Lugano Cup in late September. Allow for a two-week recovery period from the World Championships, and reduce intensity of workouts in the week approaching the Lugano. During the remaining weeks, follow the recommended schedule below.

Sunday 20 miles; 8:15-8:30 per mile pace.

Monday 1 hour at easy pace.

Tuesday VO_2 max intervals, using 1,000m efforts. (Refer to Table B on page 60 to determine pace, number of repetitions and rest periods.)

Wednesday 1 hour at easy pace.
Thursday 90:00 at medium pace.
Friday 1 hour at easy pace.
Saturday Threshold intervals: 2 X 5,000m at pace
per Table A.
Total mileage: 55

Weekly Training Schedule for Each Month of the Third Year
50 Kilometer Time Goal: 3:50.00

November:
Sunday 20 miles; 9:00 per mile pace. One Sunday
during the month, switch to 25 miles;
10:00 per mile pace.
Monday 1 hour at medium pace.
Tuesday 25km; 9:00 per mile pace.
Wednesday 10 miles; 8:30 per mile pace.
Thursday 25km; 8:45 per mile pace.
Friday 1 hour at easy pace.
Saturday 7 miles; 8:30 per mile pace.
Total mileage: 80

December:
Sunday 50km; 4:30.00. One Sunday during the
month, switch to 35km; sub-8:30 per
mile pace.
Monday 1 hour at easy pace.
Tuesday 25km; 9:00 per mile pace.
Wednesday 10 miles; 8:30 per mile pace.
Thursday 30km; 8:45 per mile pace.
Friday 90:00 at medium pace.
Saturday 15km; 8:30 per mile pace.
Total mileage: 100

January:
Sunday 50 km; sub-4:20.00. One Sunday during
the month, switch to 35km; sub-8:30 per
mile pace.
Monday 2 hours at easy pace, increasing speed for
the final 30:00.
Tuesday 25km; 8:45 per mile pace.
Wednesday 10 miles; 8:30 per mile pace.
Thursday 30km; 8:45 per mile pace.

Friday   90:00; fartlek workout for the final hour, using long efforts.

Saturday   15km; 8:00 per mile pace.

Total mileage: 120

February:

Repeat January's schedule, increasing the pace of workouts slightly as the weeks progress.

March:

Sunday   50km; sub-4:15.00; One Sunday during the month, switch to 20 miles; 8:15 per mile pace.

Monday   10 miles; 8:30-9:00 per mile pace.

Tuesday   25km; 8:30 per mile pace.

Wednesday   Threshold intervals; choose from 7 X 3,000m or 4 X 5,000m. (Refer to Table A on page 59 to determine pace and rest periods.)

Thursday   15 miles, increasing speed every 5 miles.

Friday   2 hours at easy pace.

Saturday   Threshold intervals: 3 X 5,000m at pace per Table A.

Total mileage: 105

April:

Sunday   50km; sub-4:30. One Sunday during the month, switch to 20 miles; 8:15 per mile pace.

Monday   7 miles; 8:00 per mile pace.

Tuesday   20km; 8:15 per mile pace.

Wednesday   25km; 8:30 per mile pace.

Thursday   VO$_2$ max intervals, using 1 mile efforts. (Refer to Table B on page 60 to determine pace, number of repetitions and rest periods.)

Friday   1 hour at easy pace.

Saturday   Threshold intervals: 3 X 5000m at pace per Table A.

Total mileage: 95

May:

Sunday   20 miles; sub-8:00 per mile pace.

Monday   7 miles at medium pace.

Tuesday   20km; 8:20 per mile pace.

Wednesday   Threshold intervals at 50km target race

pace; choose from 6 X 3,000m or
3 X 5,000m.
Thursday   1 hour at easy pace.
Friday   20km; 8:00 per mile pace.
Saturday   10 X 1 mile at 50km target race pace,
with 2:00 rest periods.
Total mileage: 85

June:

Olympic trials. Reduce the intensity of workouts in
the week before Trials, allow one week for recovery
time after the competition, and then resume schedule.
Sunday   35km; sub-8:00 per mile pace.
Monday   1 hour at easy pace.
Tuesday   VO₂ max intervals, using 1 mile efforts.
(Refer to Table B to determine pace,
number of repetitions and rest periods.)
Wednesday   90:00 at medium pace.
Thursday   1 hour at easy pace.
Friday   Economy intervals, using 800m efforts
at pace per Table C.
Saturday   1 hour at easy pace.
Total mileage: 75

July:

Repeat June's schedule, decreasing distance and
increasing pace of interval workouts as Olympic
games approach. As usual, use economy workouts for
no more than 8 consecutive weeks.

Chapter X

Racing

Rest before a major competition is essential. Elements broken down by training must be given time to renew; red blood cells must be regenerated to carry maximum oxygen; and glycogen supplies must be replenished.

The amount of time required for this renewal to take place varies from individual to individual and also depends upon the training background. But, as is the case with most training questions, it is best to err on the side of caution and take ample rest time. Assuming that athletes have followed a schedule similar to those given earlier, they should taper off the recommended training program for several days, completing approximately $\frac{2}{3}$ of the regular program and follow with two full days of rest before competition. The walker should be in the best possible condition one week before the race, instead of feeling that a few last-minute workouts will make the difference. During the last two days, some light strolling and the special race walking mobility routines will help to prevent any muscle tightening.

Mental Factors

The proper pre-race attitude is one of excitement. Excitement, as well as anticipation of the results of a strong racing effort, will create a healthy mental atmosphere and allows walkers to take advantage of their training.

Fear, the other emotion most often experienced by athletes before major competitions, is, of course, less desirable. Fear leads to self-doubt, which has been clinically proven to rob the body of strength and stamina. Many tactics have been reported to help athletes deal with fear, ranging from self-hypnosis to listening to music. The individual walker must learn how best to cope with his or her own fears about the race.

Athletes often complain of feelings of lassitude and lethargy during the last few hours before a race. These feelings actually should be viewed as *positive* factors, because such emotions are physical signs that the body is relaxing itself in preparation for a major effort.

The Race

Judging Factors

Judging should be a major influence in a walker's racing strategy. The race does not always go to the swiftest, the strongest. Each of these athletes can fall prey to a red flag. There are, however, practical steps that a competitor can take to minimize the risk of being disqualified.

Even walkers with basically sound technique should be careful around the judges. Passing several competitors at once, for instance, draws judging attention. Walkers should either pass between judging stations or pass more gradually.

Because a good chief judge will pull some of the other judges away from the course to concentrate on the last few dozen meters of a race, it is best to pass competitors earlier in the course, rather than save energy for a last-second burst of power near the finish line. By making an early move, you not only reduce the risk of drawing attention to yourself, but force others to make *their* moves to overtake you in these last closely-judged few meters.

Many walkers with sloppy technique employ a tactic that is growing more and more popular; these athletes "hide" in the middle of a large pack, ignore proper technique and try to stay out of the judges' sight. This tactic, while sounding reliable in theory if the principles of decency and fair play are thrown aside, is usually not effective. Hiding walkers will eventually have to break out of the pack and will have difficulty adjusting to legal technique at that point.

When warned during a race, the proper reaction is one of caution and relaxing to improve technique. Many walkers instead react with anger and frustration, and may actually increase their pace. These emotions contribute to tension, and shaky technique will become worse. If warnings persist, it is certainly far preferable to slow down and finish the race, rather than completely lose the competition through disqualification.

Walkers can also maximize the chances that their competitors who are walking poorly will be disqualified.

Fair walkers can exert bursts of speed in front of the judges, forcing these opponents to increase their tempo and risk disqualification, or fall back. Athletes with sound technique should make every effort not to let shaky walkers use them as "shields" in front of the judges. Simply pulling clear from these competitors will give officials a chance to spot illegal technique.

Pace Factors

The most efficient pace for any race is a consistent one, which avoids lactacid states for as long as possible. If walkers begin a race using a pace too close to their maximum speeds, they immediately will begin working

The walker in the above photograph demonstrates classic overstriding at the end of a high-speed race: head down, facial tension, leading arm high and leading leg straightening prematurely. This walker will probably lose contact in the next fraction of a second, and is incurring dangerous jarring as a result of landing with a locked knee. (Photo by Wayne Glusker.)

near their VO$_2$ max state and create lactacids. These lactacids will not decrease unless the pace is slowed considerably or the walker stops, and neither is a desirable action. It is more likely that the competitor will try to continue at the same tempo, resulting in increasing discomfort and a loss of control in technique. Rapid panting and heavy perspiration are warning signs that the walker is rapidly creating lactacids. These signs should be heeded, no matter how energetic the walker may be feeling otherwise.

Another advantage of a starting pace well below maximum speed is to trigger the body's fuel system to burn fats for energy, instead of the limited glycogen supplies. A good warmup will also start the body on this desirable fat-burning process, as long as the warmup is done in the aerobic state.

Varying the pace during the race will also create excess lactacids. If walkers are being passed during a race, they should respond with a long surge rather than with a quick acceleration, which creates a sudden demand for oxygen and energy supplies. Similarly, walkers should devote energy to long surges during the latter stages of a race, rather than holding back and relying on a last-minute sprint to the finish.

An ideal walking race might develop with the following sequence of events:

You start out in the middle of the pack, at a fast, challenging tempo, but working in the aerobic state. You are tiring, but exhilarated. The walkers who started too fast and have been ahead begin to tire, fall behind and draw warnings.

At mid-race, you receive a warning, but use it as a reminder to relax and smooth out your technique. Because you have energy reserves, it is possible to make these adjustments and actually increase your tempo.

As the race draws to a close, you begin a long surge, passing several competitors whose poor pace judgement has left them exhausted. Approaching the finish line, you pass one competitor who has led much of the way but is now completely spent, still recovering from a fast start. The walker has drawn numerous warnings, which contributes to increasing stress. You cross the finish line in second position, only to learn that the apparent winner has been disqualified in the last few meters in an effort to stay ahead of you.

Chapter XI

Injury Prevention and Treatment

Overexertion, or too much training and not enough rest, is the main cause of injuries in distance athletics. It is easy to sympathize with an athlete whose overzealousness results in injury, and just as easy to curse at an unjust world when months of training are lost due to an injury. However, walkers must learn to deal realistically with injuries, to devote the training time to building strength to avoid them, and handle an injury by stopping or reducing training and seeking treatment. Few, if any injuries will improve on their own if the training load is not decreased. Beginning treatment immediately after the onset of an injury significantly reduces to time that will be lost from training.

Over the years, an athlete must develop sensitivity to the possible symptoms of injury and learn to differentiate serious problems from the normal aches and pains of training. For example, a sharp pain in the shins, pain under the kneecap or sharp pain in the arch may indicate the possibility of a severe injury. Likewise, a sore throat, sudden weight loss or lassitude when waking in the morning reveal that the body may be overstressed and in danger of some type of breakdown.

Although it is best to seek out a competent sports physician, a limited amount of self-diagnosis and treatment is possible for some minor injuries. Follow these guidelines:

- Ice massage is the best all-around treatment for reducing swelling and pain, and is most effective when used immediately after workouts and before going to bed. For small painful areas, hold a few chopped-up ice cubes in a cloth and massage directly over the injured area for at least 15 minutes at a time. When a large area such as the knee or hamstring muscle is injured, holding an ice bag

directly over the area, rather than ice massage,
yields the best results.
* The use of heat is more difficult to monitor;
applying heat to a sore area may do as much harm
as good, especially if swelling is present.
* Aspirin therapy can be productive. Taking two
aspirin every four hours immediately after
workouts can help reduce swelling and pain. Be sure
to drink plenty of water when you take aspirin.
* Certain flexibility and range-of-motion exercises
can be helpful, especially after the first days of pain
have passed and swelling has subsided. Refer to the
exercises in "Training for Flexibility."

Common Race Walking Injuries, Treatment and Prevention

Shin Splints

Shin splints is a term used to describe shin pain, but
usually refers to pain over the anterior area of the shin just
above the top of the ankle joint. This common injury,
although likely to occur during all stages of an athlete's
career, most often affects walkers in the early phases of
speed training. Thus, walkers should use caution when
incorporating speed work into their training schedule,
particularly after several months of base work. A good
warm-up, as well as flexibility exercises that increase the
range of motion in the shins, are excellent preventive
measures for shin splints.

Ice massage and elevating the foot are the most
effective treatments that walkers can perform on their
own. One athlete suffering from shin pains kept her foot on
her desktop while at work, and sat on the floor in the back
of an airplane on the way to a meet in order to keep her foot
elevated as much as possible. The injured area must be
elevated higher than the heart.

Rest is also essential for healing shin troubles.
Because shin pain can be intense, convincing an athlete to
rest is usually not difficult. If training in spite of shin
splints *is* necessary, avoid walking on hills, which places
extra strain on the shins. Speed work should also be
reduced drastically.

Knee Pain

Chrondomalasia patella, a common term for knee
pain, literally means "chronic pain." In race walking, the
final straightening phase of the knee action very often

brings on this pain, which in many cases is due to muscle weakness or imbalance in the quadraceps.

Several exercises can increase the muscle strength to the level required by race walking. Seek advice from a physical trainer and locate weight equipment. Nautilus lifting equipment is superb for isolating the muscles that need strengthening to combat chrondomalacia. Packing the knee in ice is the most effective pain relief treatment.

Other Injuries

As with any distance athlete, serious race walkers may suffer from a variety of injuries. Aside from shin splints and knee pain, most race walking injuries are similar to those suffered by distance runners. Fortunately, good treatment and expert trainers are usually available due to the popularity of running.

There are several general rules that a race walker or any distance athlete should keep in mind to avoid these "generic" injuries.

- Especially when performing speed work, a good warm-up, consisting of at least two miles of strolling and a few hard 100 meter sprints, is essential and downright crucial during early season workouts and in colder weather. If you have a tendency toward a specific injury, incorporate warm-up exercises into your routine that are specifically designed to prevent this injury.
- A good rule of thumb for preventing illnesses when training is to measure your pulse rate each morning while still in bed. Any deviation of more than 10 percent from the regular rate should be viewed as a sign that the body is in an overstressed condition. The workout load should be reduced and absolutely no time trials or speed work should be performed.
- When the chance of injury is present, always tend towards too little training. If you are worried about an ache or pain, reduce the intensity of the day's workout. One light day will not threaten your overall progression, but an injury can curtail or even cancel an entire season— or career!
- Do not fall into the trap of using worn or cheap shoes, especially if you have a tendency to get any type of leg injuries.
- Efficient technique will distribute the stress of training and racing evenly throughout the body, lessening the chances of an injury or overloading in a particular joint or muscle group.

Chapter XII

Nutrition

Several books have been written on the controversial subject of nutrition for athletes. Despite the scientific basis of much nutritional advice, many champion distance athletes flaunt their poor nutritional habits. *Advanced Race Walking* will skirt this controversial area by concentrating on some basic and widely-accepted nutritional advice that supports other concepts in this book.

During the training stage when progressive adaptation occurs, the body cannot build certain kinds of strength without proper nutrition. Iron is necessary to replace red blood cells destroyed in training and to build new cells to overcompensate. The body needs 12 to 15 milligrams of iron daily, and even greater amounts if you are female. Iron is common in many foods, especially red meat. Red meat should be eaten at least twice per week to ensure that the body receives enough iron and amino acids that help produce red blood cells. However, because they can be hard to digest, red meats and protein should be avoided for a period of 24 hours before a hard race or training session.

Supplements which aid the production of red blood cells include Vitamin B6, magnesium, folic acid and especially Vitamin E. Vitamin E seems to be valuable to the distance athlete in other ways also; it appears to act as a vasodilator, opening the small arteries that carry blood to the muscles. Distance athletes, who must often train in cold, wet weather and are often overstressed, can be especially vulnerable to colds and respiratory ailments. Vitamin C (3,000 units) should be taken daily to build resistance to these ailments.

Carbohydrate loading, which is commonly practiced by athletes preparing for a big race, is not as useful in building carbohydrate reserves over a long period of time. In carbohydrate loading, glycogen reserves first are depleted through a long workout of 35 kilometers or longer. Then the athlete maintains a diet which is low in carbohydrates for three or four days, followed by a high carbohydrate diet. This program, when targeted at a specific event, builds the body's glycogen reserves for a short time. The most effective way to build glycogen reserves over an entire season is to eat meals high in carbohydrates after long workouts, avoiding fats and proteins at that time.

During the racing season, other considerations come into play. It has been proven that caffeine facilitates the body's use of fats for energy. Yet, caffeine also has side effects. Therefore walkers should experiment with this stimulant in conjunction with distance workouts to ensure that stomach difficulties do not result.

Alcohol may or may not interfere with proper utilization of glycogen in the liver. Although research is inconclusive, excessive use of alcohol definitely interferes with an athlete's management of diet and rest, and should be avoided as much as possible, especially during the peak racing season.

The most basic advice on nutrition possibly may prove to be the most valuable: be sure to drink at least eight glasses of water each day during training and racing. Dehydration often contributes to an athlete's inability to recover from hard workouts and racing.

Chapter XIII

Judging

While not everyone will agree that race walking is the most difficult event in track and field athletics, everyone should agree that race walking judging is certainly the most difficult officiating assignment. Yet the future of the sport depends upon correct, consistent and fair judging. Unless the rules of the sport are rewritten to allow an obvious *flight phase*, judges must continue to develop their ability to control the superbly trained, highly competitive athletes who simply are too strong to walk legally at high speed. Although this rewriting has been discussed, it is not likely to occur.

The first assignments of novice judges are likely to involve walkers whose abilities more or less match their own, since beginning judges should not be officiating events where the best walkers are competing. The events which they *are* likely to judge, such as local 10 kilometer road races or the Junior Olympics, are much easier to judge than major races. In other words, the skill of the walkers will more or less equal that of their judges, and lifting and creeping will not be difficult to detect. Events such as the national championships or trials races require judges who are competent in detecting marginal rule violations, which they might not have possessed the skill to spot earlier in their judging careers.

If you are considering beginning a career in judging, there are certain practical measures you can take to develop expertise:

- Officiate as many races as you can, and compare your calls to those of more experienced judges. Find the reasons behind calls which may have differed from your own.
- View films of races which you have judged, especially if the action was filmed in the area where you were judging. But remember: marginal lifting is

detectable only on film and the rules read "as detected by the human eye." Do not be discouraged if race films reveal very marginal lifting that you did not detect.

- Get a copy of the excellent judges' handbook available through the Athletics Congress.
- Always give the walker the benefit of the doubt in the case of marginal calls. Do not submit a card until you are sure that one is deserved. Warnings should be used in borderline situations.
- Be sure that the set of rules and judging procedures that you are using is up-to-date. The rules do change periodically and you must be aware of these changes in order to judge correctly.

A Short Course on Judging Procedure

Study these steps, both technical and non-technical, which should be followed when judging an important race walking event:

1. The judges meet before the start of the race and elect a "chief judge." All judges should be suitably attired, especially if the race is held as part of a major track and field meet. Many major meets supply uniforms, or at least shirts. Local T.A.C. officials' associations may also supply uniforms.
2. Each judge must carry a two-sided paddle, one side with the symbol for "lifting" ($\wedge\!\wedge\!\wedge$) and the other side with the symbol for "creeping" ($\rangle$). The judge must also have an ample supply of red disqualification cards, a pencil or pen and a sheet for recording warnings.
3. The chief judge positions the other judges around a track or along a road course. There should be no more than six judges, including the chief judge, at a track event.
4. The chief judge either can walk around the course or remain in one place; a messenger should bring the other judges' disqualification cards to the chief judge in either case. Rapid communication is vital, because walkers who have received three red cards should be pulled from the race as soon as possible or they may influence other competitors. For this reason, the runners should be equipped with

bicycles if the event is on a road in order to travel from judge to judge quickly.

5. A recorder must keep count of the disqualification cards as fast as they are brought in by the runners. If the recorder informs the chief judge that three red cards have been turned in for a certain walker, the chief judge double-checks these cards, and notifies the walker of the disqualification card with a red flag. Under the present rules, only the chief judge can notify a walker that he or she is disqualified. The walker immediately leaves the course and removes his/her number.

6. By the present I.A.A.F. rules, individual judges may issue only warnings. They may give a warning before writing a disqualification card, but this is not required. The warning should be issued by holding out the paddle, indicating the possible penalty, and loudly announcing the number of the competitor who is receiving the call.

   Making eye contact with a walker is a good way to ensure that the athlete understands that he or she is the object of the call. This is doubly important if the walker is racing in a pack. The individual judges do not give their warning calls to the messenger to deliver to the chief judge, but keep count of these calls on their own recording sheet. After the race, the red cards should be double-checked again, to ensure that all walkers who received three cards have been disqualified.

7. As the race draws to its finish, the chief judge must be sure that at least three judges are present at the finish line. A walker who has received no red cards up to this point may break into a full-fledged illegal sprint in the last 100 meters and move up several places. If only two judges are present, their two red cards will not suffice to remove the walker from the race.

8. At a preappointed time following the race, all judges should meet away from the track and review their individual warning calls and compare dis-qualification cards. Nothing which is discussed at this time can change the outcome of the race, but such meetings are vitally important to maintaining fair and consistent judging.

The above points are a small sample of judging

practices. I would like to make a few less official observations and offer advice to judges, based on 10 years of judging at the local, national, and international level.

- "If you can't stand the heat, get out of the kitchen." Walkers may physically threaten you and irate parents may pour out of the stands, but keep the sport's integrity alive and make the calls which you believe in.
- On the other hand, give the benefit of the doubt to the athlete, and be aware if your calls are consistently out of line with the other judges. The sport is continually progressing, and do not be unwilling to change your standards if you are frequently too strict or too lenient in your calls.
- Be alert for walkers who stay hidden in the middle of packs, resting with poor form and preparing themselves for an all-out effort at the finish.
- If you continually give warnings or dis-qualification cards to a certain walker, be sure that these calls do not stem from a particular prejudice against this athlete. If a walker's style is unacceptable in your opinion, try to help the athlete improve or at least refer him or her to a coach whom you both respect. Nothing is more frustrating to athletes than knowing that a certain judge will invariably give them a call.
- Do not be intimidated by reports that athletes were lifting in a race you were judging, and you did not make calls. Reviewing films after races by other athletes is dangerous, especially if they were beaten by an athlete clearly "way off the ground." Again, such observations are immaterial, when the rule reads "as viewed by the human eye." On the other hand, do not totally ignore such reports. If the films show that someone was indeed lifting flagrantly, you may not have been judging with the proper strictness.

Conclusion

Jerzy Hausleber, the widely respected and successful coach of the Mexican National Race Walking Team, once remarked to me that the problem with U.S. race walkers was that they spend all of their time talking about technique and training, and not enough time actually *doing* the training. The way to succeed, he said, was to stop talking and "get out and do it." There is a lot of truth in Hausleber's advice. The preceding pages have provided you with the most advanced and up-to-date technical knowledge available. Now it's up to you.

Digest all of the information, take a lab test to determine your own VO_2 max and threshold level, chart out your own three-year training program, but in the end, do not neglect to put this preparation into practice on the road and track. It can be frustrating, tedious, unrewarding at times— but in the end, success in competitive race walking is worth every sore muscle, every drop of sweat. Get out and do it!

Glossary

Aerobic Training— Training which is performed at a pulse rate and effort level that allows for an adequate supply of oxygen to the body. Because the body is constantly supplied with sufficient oxygen during aerobic training, the athlete will not experience the pain and fatigue which typically accompany more taxing workouts. For most athletes, the upper pulse rate of aerobic training is approximately 130 beats per minute.

Anaerobic Threshold— The pulse rate at which the body moves from an aerobic to an anaerobic state. Training is often most efficient when performed in the upper ranges between the aerobic and anaerobic states, at a pulse rate range around 150 beats per minute.

Anaerobic Training— Training which is performed at a pulse rate and effort level that deprives the body of a sufficient supply of oxygen, causing pain and fatigue. For most athletes, the pulse rate of anaerobic training is above 150 beats per minute

The Athletics Congress (TAC)— The governing body for track and field athletics in the United States. TAC supplies the funding and the volunteer officials that maintain the sport of race walking.

Ballistic Stretching— Exercises designed to increase the flexibility of specified areas of the body by way of a series of repetitive movements, which force these areas beyond their usual stretching limits. Because this form of stretching increases the risk of injury, it is not recommended

Carbohydrate Loading— A way of maximizing the body's store of glycogen for use during an endurance event. The standard process of carbohydrate loading is accomplished through several steps: the athlete should first deplete the body's glycogen supply through a hard race or training session of at least 90 minutes in duration; maintain a diet of mainly protein foods for three days; and maintain a diet of primarily carbohydrate-loaded foods in the following three days, in preparation for the race on the seventh day.

Chrondomalasia Patella— Chronic knee pain which is often of undetermined origin. Distance athletes frequently suffer from this condition.

Circumduction— An incorrect body movement most often seen in race walking when the foot of the advancing leg swings wide and the knee hyperextends inward. This common fault in technique can cause a variety of leg injuries.

Creeping— The failure to straighten the knee of the supporting leg as it passes under the body's center during race walking. Race walkers can be disqualified for the creeping violation.

Depletion Training— Training in which the body is driven to the point where all glycogen reserves have been expended for energy. This training forces the body through a process of adaptation to increase its supply of glycogen for future training and racing situations. The body is depleted of glycogen after approximately 90 minutes of training or racing in the anaerobic state or approximately 20 miles of work in the aerobic state.

Double Contact Phase— The period during a race walker's stride in which both feet are on the ground. This phase occurs when the heel of the advancing foot has made contact with the ground before the toe of the rear foot has left the ground. This period is also known as the double support phase.

Dynamic Flexibility— The ability to stretch certain muscles and connective tissue groups throughout a wide range of motion. Dynamic flexibility requires static flexibility plus relaxation.

Economy Training— High-speed interval training. Economy workouts are aimed at improving speed technique and reducing the body's output of lactic acid at high speeds.

Fartlek— A Swedish word meaning "speed play." Fartlek workouts involve speed training that incorporates hard efforts of walking and walking recovery periods, both of varying distances. This type of workout is often used during the base and transition periods of a training cycle in order to maintain speed ability.

Fast Twitch Muscle Tissue– The tissue which reacts to the brain's command for rapid contractions to produce speed. Individuals are born with a preponderance of either fast or slow twitch muscle fibers. The amount of fast twitch versus slow twitch muscle tissue determines an athlete's ultimate leg speed.

Flight Phase– The period of lifting when both feet are off the ground and the walker is gaining extra distance as a result.

Glucose– A substance which is primarily obtained from the starches and sugars of carbohydrates. Once it reaches the muscle cells, glucose is broken down into carbon dioxide, water and muscle energy. During anaerobic training, when the body is not receiving an adequate supply of oxygen, lactic acids are formed simultaneously with glucose.

Glycogen– The body's energy supply. Glycogen is stored in the muscles and liver, ready to be changed to glucose as needed for energy during exercise.

International Amateur Athletic Federation (IAAF)– The international governing body for track and field athletics. The IAAF dictates all rules of race walking as well as the conduct of international walking races.

Intervals– Workouts consisting of a series of hard walking efforts over a predetermined distance at a set pace, followed by rest periods. These workouts are used to improve VO_2 max, raise the anaerobic threshold and/or improve economy.

Isometrics– A technique of building strength by exerting force against an immobile object. Isometric training is not effective in building the type of endurance strength that is most desirable for distance athletes.

Lactacid Stage– The phase during anaerobic training in which lactic acids accumulate. Because the formation of lactic acids leads to pain and a loss of muscle control, the body can work for only a limited period of time in this state.

Lactic Acid– A by-product of glucose production. A build-up of lactic acid occurs rapidly during anaerobic training, causing pain and stiffness in the muscles.

Lifting– The failure to maintain contact with the ground during race walking or sustain the action known as the double contact phase. Lifting occurs when the heel of the advancing foot has not made contact with the ground before the toe of the rear foot has been snatched away. Race walkers can be disqualified for the lifting violation.

Orthotics— Custom-designed arch supports, usually cast and constructed by a podiatrist, which can aid in overcoming pronation.

Proprioceptive Neuromuscular Facilitation (PNF) Stretching Techniques— The most recent method of stretching employed by athletes. PNF exercises involve repetitive stretches and tension of the same muscle group, which alters the nervous system's influence on the muscles. These techniques are particularly effective in improving those muscles that do not respond well to standard stretching techniques.

Progressive Stress Adaptation— The basis of modern athletic training first described by Dr. Hans Selye in his classic work, *The Stress of Life*. By Selye's principles, an athlete should stress his or her body during training in order to adapt to the current level of exertion, and handle even greater workloads of similar stress in the future.

Pronation— An injury-causing condition of the feet and ankles in which the supporting foot collapses inwards when bearing weight. Several factors can contribute to pronation, including weak arches, tight calf muscles and structural deficiencies. The proper exercises and custom-built orthotics can aid in correcting this condition.

Static Flexibility— The ability to stretch certain muscles and connective tissue through a limited range of motion.

Strike Rate— The number of steps taken by a walker during a designated period of time, i.e., the number of steps per second. An athlete's strike rate serves as an accurate definition of leg speed.

Swayback— A common term for an inward curve of the lower spine. Swayback is a frequent condition among race wakers, resulting from weak abdominal muscles and a tight lower back. Many injuries and style problems stem from this condition.

Threshold Training— The term used in this book to describe longer interval workouts at a pace near target race pace. Tempo workouts are designed to improve the body's ability to work near the VO_2 max rate over a longer period of time.

VO_2 Max (Maximum Volume of Oxygen)— The maximum amount of oxygen that the body can carry. Because the body can only work at VO_2 max for a short period of time, this capacity determines an athlete's true endurance potential. VO_2 max can be improved with proper training and by losing excess body fat.

References

Algoni, Frank. *Race Walking Technique*, unpublished, Dearborn Heights, Michigan, 1985.

Clippinger-Robertson, Karen. "Abdominal Stength For Race Walkers," unpublished, Seattle, Washington, 1986.

Clippinger-Robertson, Karen. "Flexibility For Race Walkers," unpublished, Seattle, Washington, 1986.

Daniels, Jack. "Over and Out," *Runner's World*, July 1986.

Daniels, Jack. "Testing of Elite Race Walkers," unpublished, Seattle, Washington, 1986.

Hausleber, Jerzy, personal communication, 1978.

Hopkins, Julian. *Race Walking*, British Amateur Athletic Board, London, England, 1977.

Kamin, et al, translated by R.W. Snyder. "Two Styles of Race Walking: Which One is Better?" Translated by R.W. Snyder, *Legkaia atletika*, v.12, 1979.

Londree, Ben. "The Use of Labratory Test Results With Long Distance Runners," *Sports Medicine*, v.3, 1986.

Murry, et al. "Kinematic and Electromyographic Patterns of Olympic Race Walkers," *The American Journal of Sports Medicine*, V.11, 1983.

Nelson, Cordner. *Advanced Running Book*, Runner's World Books, Mountain View, California, 1983.

Robertson, John, M.D., personal correspondence, 1987.

Rudow, Martin. *Race Walking*, World Publications, Mountain View, California, 1974.